DK GARDEN GUIDES

ROSES

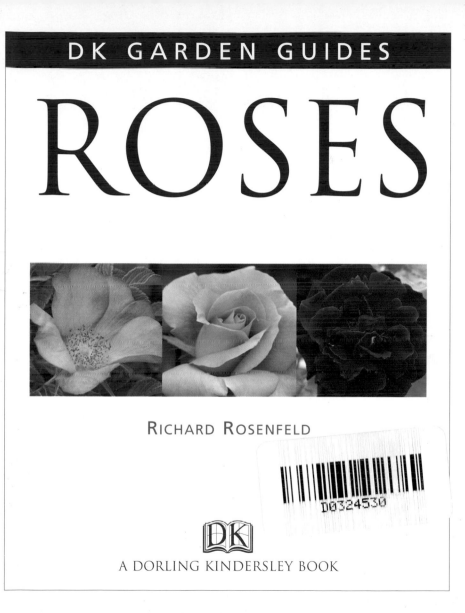

RICHARD ROSENFELD

DK

A DORLING KINDERSLEY BOOK

**LONDON, NEW YORK,
MUNICH, MELBOURNE, DELHI**

Series Editor Helen Fewster
Series Art Editor Alison Donovan
Art Editor Ann Thompson
Designer Rachael Smith
Editor Jane Simmonds
Managing Editor Anna Kruger
Managing Art Editor Lee Griffiths
Consultant Louise Abbott
DTP Designer Louise Waller
Media Resources Lucy Claxton
Picture Research Juliet Duff
Production Controller Mandy Inness

First published in Great Britain in 2003 by
Dorling Kindersley Limited
80 Strand, London, WC2R ORL
A Penguin company

Copyright © 2003
Dorling Kindersley Limited, London

A CIP catalogue record for this book is available
from the British Library
ISBN 0 7513 3876 1

Colour reproduction by Colourscan, Singapore
Printed and bound by Printer Trento, Italy

see our complete catalogue at
www.dk.com

Gardening with roses

ROSES CAN BE GROWN in a fantastic range of gardens from the smart to the wild. They can be used as manicured, elegant shrubs or as standards, with globes of flowers at the top of single, upright stems. They make superb stand-alone features in the middle of a lawn and gap-fillers in borders, as well as excellent flowering hedges. Climbers and ramblers can be let loose into the tops of trees. And you have a choice of eight different flower shapes, including tight, petal packed balls ("pompons") and the stylish "high-centred" with a smart tip in the middle.

When compiling a list of "must-have" roses, make sure that each has a different feature. For good scent, try GERTRUDE JEKYLL or 'Fantin-Latour'. You can even choose a quick colour-change rose, like *Rosa* x *odorata* 'Mutabilis'. The flowers start copper-yellow, change to pink, and end up copper-crimson, and you get all three colours simultaneously because new buds keep on coming. If you have room go for *Rosa sericea* subsp. *omeiensis* f. *pteracantha*. Its pointy thorns are flat, red, and translucent. But the most important point when choosing a rose is to match its shape, vigour, and behaviour to the style of your garden design.

Roses in small capitals (for example, KENT) denote recognised trade names used by rose suppliers.

◀ **HERITAGE brightens up** borders with its lemon-scented, light pink flowers.

▶ **Choose roses** with excellent hips because they add bright colours after the flowers.

A deep pink rose mingles well with *Geranium* x *oxonianum* 'Wargrave Pink'.

Right rose, right garden

Formal gardens invariably need well-behaved roses with a balanced shape (or ones that can be pruned to keep them orderly) and a uniform height when grown in blocks, while cottage gardens are best for roses with a wilder, more rampant look that adds to the hazy, meandering flow. And in both formal and informal gardens, all sorts of roses can be grown among perennials and other shrubs as dominant, eye-catching features or exceptionally useful fillers. The day of the dedicated rose garden might be over but as a combination plant it can't be beaten.

Colourful divides

Rose hedges or divides can also be used in formal and informal gardens, and the choice of plants is huge from knee-high bushes for small areas to head-high shrubs for large spaces. Alternatively, try climbers with a long flowering season trained along horizontal wires fixed to sturdy wooden posts, checking that the roses' growth statistics roughly coincide with the size of the screen.

Ground-cover, standard, and climbing roses

Ground-cover roses rarely completely block out the weeds, but they do shoot outwards at a low height, and are good fun at the edge of a pond or spreading down a bank in a wild garden.

Standards go the opposite way, creating a ball of flowers on top of a long, thin leg. They can be used to encircle a pond, stand at the back of

This subtle blend of colours uses *Rosa* Paul Shirville and sky-blue love-in-a-mist.

Climbing roses and vines combine to create an elegant and colourful walkway.

Small-scale gardening

Plenty of roses can also be grown in tubs, half-barrels, and large pots, and in decent-sized gaps in patios. The smallest roses are called patio or miniature roses, with the miniatures generally being up to 45cm (18in) high, and the patio roses slightly taller. Usually airy and twiggy, they need a small-scale design where they can be clearly seen.

The standard *Rosa* 'Little White Pet' provides a gentle focal point with its ball of flowers.

Pruning

Whichever roses you buy, do not be alarmed by the pruning. You can be as fussy or relaxed as you like. Some roses have even survived sessions with a hedge trimmer and still performed incredibly well. But

a border, or mark the beginning of a very grand path, and they keep the eye moving around.

But for the best aerial show you do need climbers and ramblers. For the ultimate climber try *Rosa mulliganii*, a rampant wild white rose. And try one with a beautiful high-pointed flower, like 'Guinée'. The colour is deep, dark, and red, and the rich scent gulps straight to the lungs.

Patio roses are ideal for tubs, and create a superb show with busy Lizzies.

you must always get rid of the three "Ds", the diseased, dead, and damaged wood. After that, tailor your regime to match your and your roses' needs and your garden design. For a smart look, prune bushy roses hard to lick them into shape. In cottage gardens, a skimpy trim is fine. You decide what goes.

Types of roses

OVER CENTURIES OF CULTIVATION, roses have been divided into types according to how they grow, when they flower, and how they need to be pruned. Knowing the characteristics of each type helps you choose which you need – from a modern, long-flowering one for a formal border to a wild rose for easy growth in an informal garden.

Old garden roses

There are many different kinds of old garden rose. They vary enormously but generally have one superb flowering period in midsummer, many with a fantastic rich scent and strong colour. They can be grown in borders or as feature plants.

◀ **Alba rose**
A typical Alba rose, *R. x alba* 'Alba Maxima' (*left*) is a free-branching, large shrub with hardly any prickles and a midsummer burst of flowers. Albas are good hedge and border plants, and need mimimal attention.

▶ **Bourbon rose**
Bourbons, like 'Zéphirine Drouhin' (*right*), are vigorous with more than one summer show of flowers, usually good scent, and a large, open shape. The stems are smooth or prickly. They are ideal in borders, against a fence, or as hedges.

◀ **Gallica rose**
The arching 'Complicata' (*left*) has one excellent display of scented flowers. It belongs to the oldest group, the Gallicas, with thorny stems, a robust constitution, and a short, bushy spread. Grow Gallicas as a hedge or in beds.

Wild roses

Also known as species roses, they invariably have one flowering period and are often perfect for hedges or when grown up into trees. They require very little attention.

▲ *R. xanthina* 'Canary Bird'
With the look of a wild rose, *R. xanthina* 'Canary Bird' has single, five-petalled blooms followed by blackish hips, and arching growth up to 3m (10ft) high. Wild roses are ideal in cottage gardens.

Modern roses

Many types of roses are included within the modern rose group, all giving a flowery display that just keeps on coming from summer to autumn. The larger, bushier kinds can be grown in rows to make hedges, garden divides, and even impenetrable barriers. There are also lower-growing ground-cover types, and miniature or patio roses that look good in pots.

▲ **Large-flowered bush rose**
DUBLIN BAY can be grown both as a large shrub and as a climber and has a long flowering period.

▲ **Cluster-flowered bush rose**
'Southampton' has the typical look of a cluster-flowered bush rose, with a mass of flowers.

▲ **Shrub rose**
Shrubs are a diverse group. 'Little White Pet' can be grown as a standard or compact shrub.

Climbing and rambling roses

The key difference between climbers and ramblers is that climbers usually have stiffer stems, and they can be trained into a strong framework from which their shoots develop. They are better on walls than ramblers, which fire up long, flexible stems from the base, making them easy to train up arches, pillars, and pergolas. Let them also climb into trees. Ramblers tend to have smaller flowers in summer clusters.

▲ **Climbing rose**
'Danse du Feu' has 2.5m (8ft) of stiff growth, and is ideal for flowering against a modest wall.

▲ **Rambling rose**
'Bobbie James' is best trained into a stout old tree, and has a mass of creamy-white flowers.

Choosing roses

ROSES ARE SOLD IN POTS or bare-root (usually from mail-order companies). The container-grown kind can be planted at any time, even in summer. Check their health when buying, and reject the diseased and feeble. Bare-root roses have been dug up from growing fields in the dormant season for planting as soon as possible.

Even covering of flower buds

Glossy, healthy-looking leaves

Strong, healthy top-growth

Container-grown rose
Check that the plant has vigorous stems and a good shape. The soil should be moist and firm. Also look for healthy roots that are not congested.

Sparse foliage

Weak shoots

Diseased leaves

Bare-root rose
Look for well-placed shoots and sturdy main roots to anchor the plant in the ground, with plenty of smaller, fibrous ones.

Strong joint between roots and stems

Thick cluster of strong roots

Spindly roots

Planting bare-rooted roses

Plant as soon as you can, in late autumn or early winter, but not in waterlogged or freezing soil. When delays do happen, keep the roses cool and frost-free, occasionally standing the roots in a bucket of water. Before planting, soak the roots for one hour and prune any dead, diseased, or damaged wood, and any crossing stems. Also trim back any damaged roots to healthy tissue. Finally, dig a wide hole that is deep enough to take the roots comfortably, and fork in plenty of well-rotted organic matter to get the roses off to a good start.

Fill in soil, firm down, and water area well

Check the planting level
Make the planting hole deep enough for the joint between the roots and stems to be 2.5cm (1in) below soil level. Check using a cane placed horizontally.

Removing suckers

Most roses are made up of the flowering top-growth and a separate, vigorous root system, onto which the top-growth has been grafted. Sometimes a shoot fires up from the roots, often with different thorns and leaves. Scrape away the soil to expose the base of the sucker, and tug it off (don't use secateurs) or energy will be channelled into this unwanted growth.

Wear gloves to grip sucker and pull out

Deadheading

When a flower starts fading, promptly snip it off. This encourages repeat-flowering roses to develop even more buds, and stops all roses from putting valuable energy into self-propagation by creating seed when it is not necessary. The exception is roses that later have an excellent show of hips – leave the flowers on or you will not get any hips at all.

◀ **Cluster-flowered roses**
Nip off the central flower, which fades first; later remove the whole cluster, cutting back to a lower bud.

▶ **Large- or single-flowered roses**
Cut back the faded flower to a healthy bud or sideshoot.

Looking after roses in containers

Some roses can easily be grown in containers. To allow the roots to spread, the pot needs to be at least 30–45cm (12–18in) deep for bush roses, or 25–35cm (10–14in) deep for miniature and patio roses. Place a layer of crocks over the drainage holes to stop the soil washing out, and then fill with John Innes No. 3 (loam-based potting compost). Water regularly, especially in hot weather.

Gap of 2.5cm (1in) between soil surface and rim to allow for watering

Pruning roses

PRUNING IS AN EXCELLENT WAY of improving on nature. It prompts vigorous, new, disease-free growth that replaces the tired and the old, creating a pleasing shape and the best possible show of flowers. It also sends shoots in the required direction (usually outwards, away from the centre). The best time to do it is in late winter when the roses are dormant.

Pruning tips

In general, prune shrubby roses quite hard in formal gardens to give a smart shape; in informal gardens you can opt for a light trim and a more carefree look. With all roses (including climbers and ramblers), when pruning for the first time, cut back to just two or three buds from the base to encourage lots of new shoots from low down. After that, follow the advice under each entry.

Correctly angled cut 5mm (¼in) above bud

Bruised tissue slow to heal

Cut slopes towards, not away from bud

Too high above bud

The perfect cut
Use clean, sharp, secateurs, and make an angled cut just above a bud (*left*). Avoid cuts like those above, which may lead to infection and dieback.

Large-flowered bush roses

Prune the main stems quite hard to an outward-pointing bud to create a balanced, shapely framework. Shape is more important for an individual rose than for several planted close together. The harder the pruning the fewer the stems, but the flowers will be quite large.

Routine pruning
As with all roses, promptly remove any dead, diseased, and damaged wood.

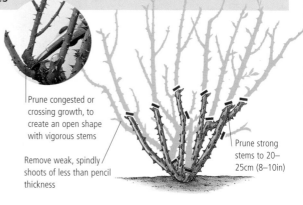

Prune congested or crossing growth, to create an open shape with vigorous stems

Remove weak, spindly shoots of less than pencil thickness

Prune strong stems to 20–25cm (8–10in)

Rambling roses

Ramblers can be let loose into tree tops, or trained against walls with their stems tied to wires. After flowering prune out some of the oldest main stems and trim the sideshoots.

Remove one in three of the oldest stems

Prune sideshoots to encourage new flowering growth

Training
Horizontal training ensures a wide spread of flowering shoots at all heights.

Climbers

To encourage climbers to flower low down and high up, train the stems horizontally so that they produce new shoots. Either tie them in if grown against a wall, or spiral them up and around a support, such as a tripod.

Cut back flowered and overlong shoots to maintain shape

Shorten some older stems to strong, young replacements

Tripod-training
Spiral the stems around the poles from low down, forcing out an even spread of flowering side-shoots along the stems. Use shortish climbers with flexible stems.

Common problems

The key to growing healthy roses is choosing healthy varieties, growing them well in first-rate, well-fed soil, and applying rose feed in spring and after flowering. If problems do strike, tackle them immediately.

▶ Powdery mildew
Often caused by poor feeding and air circulation, and dry soil. Cut off affected parts, spray with fungicide and water.

◀ Blackspot
Caused by fungus. Cut off affected parts, spray with fungicide in spring, and repeat as advised over summer.

▶ Aphids
Pick them off by hand or wait to see if the birds eat them, which they invariably do; spray as a last resort.

A-Z of Roses

A

ABRAHAM DARBY ('Auscot')

THE MAIN FLUSH OF LARGE, CUPPED FLOWERS, appearing in small clusters, comes in early summer with many more following later. They are showy apricot-pink blooms, fading with age, and have a rich, fruity scent. ABRAHAM DARBY is well known for its bushy, rounded, shapely look with strong, arching stems and dark green leaves, making it well worth a place in a border. Bear in mind its thorns when choosing its position. Prune shoots in late winter by one-half to two-thirds; harder pruning gives fewer stems with larger flowers, lighter pruning more flowering stems with smaller blooms.

PLANT PROFILE

HEIGHT 1.5m (5ft)

SPREAD 1.5m (5ft)

TYPE Shrub

HARDINESS Fully hardy

FLOWERING Summer to autumn

'Agnes'

A

DELIGHTFULLY SCENTED, LIGHT YELLOW, double flowers first appear in early summer, and there is a second, much smaller show in late summer. The wide open blooms are clearly highlighted against the slightly crinkled, dark green, glossy leaves. Vigorous and disease-free, 'Agnes' makes a graceful, bushy spray of twiggy growth, ideal in a mixed border. It is often listed with the Rugosas in rose catalogues. Prune it in late winter, shortening shoots by one-half to two-thirds. Prune harder for fewer stems with larger flowers, and more lightly for more flowering stems with smaller blooms.

PLANT PROFILE	
HEIGHT 2m (6ft)	
SPREAD 1.2m (4ft)	
TYPE Shrub	
HARDINESS Fully hardy	
FLOWERING Summer	

A | x *alba* 'Alba Maxima' Great white rose, White rose of York

AN EXCELLENT, TOUGH, VIGOROUS, disease-free shrub, this Alba rose has been popular since the 16th century, and is a must for anyone who loves old garden roses. The sweet-scented, creamy-white flowers open with a faint pink tinge, and make a gentle show against the grey-green leaves. The plant is rather gaunt and loose (untidy to some) in habit, with occasional large thorns. It is particularly good in cottage gardens. To create a large, impressive shrub, remove only diseased, dead, and damaged growth in late winter. If necessary, at the same time, give a minimal prune to help produce a balanced shape.

PLANT PROFILE

HEIGHT 2.2m (7ft)

SPREAD 1.5m (5ft)

TYPE Old garden rose

HARDINESS Fully hardy

FLOWERING Midsummer

'Albéric Barbier'

A

A BIG HIT SINCE BEING INTRODUCED over 100 years ago, 'Albéric Barbier' guarantees strong, vigorous growth. The pointed, pale yellow buds open to reveal apple-scented, 8cm (3in) wide, creamy-white flowers set against the dark green, glossy leaves. After the initial, highly impressive, early-summer display there is a further scattering of flowers. Grow it up pillars and into trees, to cover an eyesore, or on shady sites. Prune in late summer. For the first two years prune sideshoots by 8cm (3in) to a strong new shoot. Then prune up to one-third of the oldest main stems back to the ground.

PLANT PROFILE

HEIGHT To 5m (15ft)

TYPE Rambler

HARDINESS Fully hardy

FLOWERING Summer

A | 'Albertine'

AN INCREDIBLY POPULAR ROSE, 'Albertine' can be grown in various ways. Allowing space for its vigour, try it trained up a wall, against a pergola, or climbing through a tree, or let it mound up in a cottage-garden border where it will spread to 5m (15ft). The clusters of salmon-red buds open to flowers with a beautiful mix of copper and pink that are richly scented and last for three weeks. In late summer, for the first two years, prune sideshoots by 8cm (3in) to a strong shoot. In following years prune up to one-third of the oldest main stems back to ground level. Mildew can be a minor problem.

PLANT PROFILE

HEIGHT To 5m (15ft)

TYPE Rambler

HARDINESS Fully hardy

FLOWERING Midsummer

'Alchymist'

A

IT MIGHT FLOWER ONLY ONCE, in early summer, but 'Alchymist' (sometimes spelt 'Alchemist') gets high marks from most growers for its impressive show. It has strongly scented, golden-yellow to orange flowers with darker centres. Growth is vigorous, the glossy leaves are an attractive bronze, and the stems can be used as a support for a midsummer-flowering clematis. Avoid pruning for the first two years, but train new shoots into a horizontal position. From the third year prune in the autumn, after flowering, nipping back the main stems if necessary, and shortening sideshoots by two-thirds.

PLANT PROFILE

HEIGHT 4m (12ft)

TYPE Climber

HARDINESS Fully hardy

FLOWERING Early summer

A

ALEC'S RED ('Cored')

ONE OF THE BEST, small, cherry-red bush roses for the front of
the border and cut flowers, ALEC'S RED is equally impressive
when grown as a standard. Extremely popular (picking up
several awards) since being introduced in 1970, it starts
flowering in early summer and continues right through the
season. It has exquisite pointed buds and a rich, strong scent
and the leaves are on the verge of dark green. In late winter
remove all unproductive stems, and prune the remaining stems
hard to outward-facing buds at 20–25cm (8–10in). For large,
showy flowers prune harder, leaving just two or three buds.

PLANT PROFILE

HEIGHT 90cm (3ft)

SPREAD 60cm (24in)

TYPE Bush (large-flowered)

HARDINESS Fully hardy

FLOWERING Summer to autumn

ALEXANDER ('Harlex')

AN EXTREMELY VIGOROUS and disease-resistant bush rose, ALEXANDER has a lavish supply of large, showy, vermilion flowers set off by glossy, dark green leaves. It packs plenty of punch in a border, where it is a real eye-catcher, with its flowers being held up on long stems. It can also be grown in a row, making a flowery divide or head-high hedge. In late winter, remove all unproductive stems. Prune the remaining stems hard to outward-facing buds, leaving 20–25cm (8–10in) of stem above ground. This helps keep the centre of the bush clear. If you want larger blooms, prune to two or three buds.

A

PLANT PROFILE

HEIGHT	To 2m (6ft)
SPREAD	80cm (32in)
TYPE	Bush (large-flowered)
HARDINESS	Frost hardy
FLOWERING	Summer to autumn

A

'Alister Stella Gray'

EXTREMELY RELIABLE AND REPEAT-FLOWERING, this is a medium-high climber with blowsy, yolk-yellow flowers, 6cm (2½in) wide, which fade to white. The stems are thorn-free, the scent subtle, and the leaves dark green. Train it up trees, over an arch or pergola, or against a wall. The continuous show of yellow gives a good background for other climbers, including blue and red varieties of clematis. In the first two years simply train new shoots into a horizontal position. After that prune in autumn, nipping back the main stems if they outgrow their space, and shortening sideshoots by two-thirds.

PLANT PROFILE

HEIGHT To 5m (15ft)

TYPE Climber

HARDINESS Frost hardy

FLOWERING Summer to autumn

'Aloha'

A

CLIMBERS DO NOT HAVE TO SHOOT HIGH into the tree tops. This one is short and restrained, ideal for training round pillars or up average-sized walls. Everything about it is virtually perfect – the healthy, glossy foliage, fat round buds, and multi-petalled flowers with a sweet scent and a hint of orange-pink in the centre. After the first main flush of flowers, it is rarely out of bud. For the first two years train new shoots into a horizontal position, tying them into wires, or spiralling them round a pillar. From the third year, after flowering, prune by trimming the main stems as needed and shortening sideshoots.

PLANT PROFILE

HEIGHT To 3m (10ft)

TYPE Climber

HARDINESS Fully hardy

FLOWERING Summer to autumn

A 'Alpine Sunset'

THE NAME IS JUST RIGHT because the petals of 'Alpine Sunset'
mix peach, apricot, and yellow. The scented blooms are
surprisingly large, and seem to take so much out of the plant
that there can be a gap after the first flush before more appear.
But 'Alpine Sunset' does repeat flower, and excels at the front
of a border. With the flowers on short, strong stems, the whole
plant is compact, with glossy, light green leaves. In late winter
remove all unproductive stems. For large, showy flowers prune
the remaining stems to two or three buds. Otherwise prune to
an outward-facing bud 20–25cm (8–10in) from the ground.

PLANT PROFILE

HEIGHT 60cm (24in)

SPREAD 60cm (24in)

TYPE Bush (large-flowered)

HARDINESS Fully hardy

FLOWERING Summer to autumn

ALTISSIMO ('Delmur')

A

A RESTRAINED CLIMBER, ALTISSIMO can also be grown, with gentle pruning, as a 2.5m (8ft) high shrub. Either way you get flashy, bright blood-red flowers with a faint scent against dark green leaves. Extra flowers follow the first flush giving a continuous show. Training is vital: unless the new stems on a young plant are trained in a horizontal position, forcing out new branches, all the flowers may appear at the top, out of reach and sight. Pruning is not needed for the first two years. From the third year, after flowering, nip back the main stems if they are too long and shorten sideshoots by two-thirds.

PLANT PROFILE

HEIGHT	3m (10ft)
TYPE	Climber
HARDINESS	Fully hardy
FLOWERING	Summer to autumn

A AMBER QUEEN ('Harroony')

WITH A STACK OF AWARDS to its name, AMBER QUEEN is likely to get top marks at most shows, while also brightening up the garden. Short and compact in habit, it can be grown in massed displays or right at the front of a border. The scented flowers have a clean, pure colour (being nicely set off by the leathery, dark green foliage), and give a constant show all season. Prune it in late winter, cutting back the main stems to 25–45cm (10–18in) above ground level, and reducing sideshoots by about one-third of their length.

PLANT PROFILE

HEIGHT 50cm (20in)

SPREAD 60cm (24in)

TYPE Bush (cluster-flowered)

HARDINESS Fully hardy

FLOWERING Summer to autumn

'American Pillar'

A

THE OPEN FLOWERS ARE A MIX of bright, rich pink around the outside of the petals, with a white eye, and yellow central stamens. As its name suggests, grow 'American Pillar' around pillars and into trees. A big favourite in cottage gardens, it is a rampant rose and also makes a beautiful show on a pergola or rustic arch. Prune in late summer. To form the basic framework prune sideshoots by 8cm (3in) to a strong new shoot for the first two years. In the following years prune up to one-third of the oldest main stems back to ground level. The glossy, leathery leaves sometimes get a touch of mildew.

PLANT PROFILE

HEIGHT To 5m (15ft)

TYPE Rambler

HARDINESS Fully hardy

FLOWERING Midsummer

A ANGELA RIPPON ('Ocaru')

LARGE CLUSTERS OF SALMON-PINK FLOWERS, each urn-shaped and about 4cm (1½in) across, are striking against the dark green leaves of ANGELA RIPPON. This twiggy, miniature bush rose is ideal for growing in pots or in substantial gaps between paving. Its prettiness is often best isolated so that it is not lost against the great clamour of taller, summer-flowering plants. Pruning aims to force up plenty of new, vigorous growth: in late winter remove all growth apart from the strongest shoots, and then cut these back by one-third to one-half.

PLANT PROFILE	
HEIGHT	45cm (18in)
SPREAD	30cm (12in)
TYPE	Bush (miniature)
HARDINESS	Fully hardy
FLOWERING	Summer to autumn

ANISLEY DICKSON ('Dickimono')

A

A GREAT ABUNDANCE OF SMALL FLOWERS, held in clusters, keeps appearing right through summer. The flowers are neither too lipstick-bright nor too pale, but a reddish-pink. Since the supply of fattening buds is so constant, you can take as many as you want for cut flowers. The glossy leaves are dark green. It can be used as a flowering mini-hedge, or as a bush plant for the border. In late winter cut back the main stems to 25–45cm (10–18in) above the ground, and trim the sideshoots by about one-third of their length.

PLANT PROFILE	
HEIGHT	1m (3ft)
SPREAD	75cm (30in)
TYPE	Bush (cluster-flowered)
HARDINESS	Fully hardy
FLOWERING	Summer to autumn

A ANNA FORD ('Harpiccolo')

A PERFECT, SCALED-DOWN ROSE for edging, pots, and the front of a border, ANNA FORD has bright, rich orange-red flowers with yellow in the middle. It also flowers all summer, and has bushy growth and dark, glossy green leaves. Since its height of 45cm (18in) is usually borderline between the patio roses and the shorter miniatures, ANNA FORD might be listed in either group in rose catalogues. In late winter select the strongest shoots and remove the rest. Trim the remaining shoots by one-third to one-half to encourage plenty of new, vigorous flowering growth.

PLANT PROFILE

HEIGHT 45cm (18in)

SPREAD 40cm (16in)

TYPE Bush (cluster-flowered, miniature)

HARDINESS Fully hardy

FLOWERING Summer to autumn

ANNA LIVIA ('Kormetter')

A

WITH BEAUTIFUL SPRAYS OF PINK FLOWERS all summer and a pleasing, uniform shape, this rose makes bushy growth covered by leathery leaves. Though it hardly scores any points for its weak scent, ANNA LIVIA is reliably disease-free and has won a clutch of awards. It is named after James Joyce's character Anna Livia in his novel *Finnegans Wake*. Use it in pastel schemes to the front of a border where it can be clearly seen. In late winter cut back the main stems to 25–45cm (10–18in) above the ground, and reduce the sideshoots by about one-third of their length.

PLANT PROFILE	
HEIGHT	75cm (30in)
SPREAD	60cm (24in)
TYPE	Bush (cluster-flowered)
HARDINESS	Fully hardy
FLOWERING	Summer to autumn

A | ANNE HARKNESS ('Harkaramel')

IF YOU NEED A FIRST-RATE ROSE to start opening its flowers when the midsummer old garden roses have faded, this is a very good choice. ANNE HARKNESS bursts into flower in the last part of summer with spectacular flower sprays, making it excellent for a medium-high, mixed rose hedge, and ideal for arrangers. Growth is vigorous, strong, and upright, with healthy foliage. In late winter cut back the main stems to 25–45cm (10–18in) above ground level, and reduce the sideshoots by about two-thirds of their length.

PLANT PROFILE

HEIGHT 1.2m (4ft)

SPREAD 60cm (24in)

TYPE Bush (cluster-flowered)

HARDINESS Fully hardy

FLOWERING Late summer to autumn

'Arthur Bell'

A

SURPRISINGLY WELL SCENTED FOR THIS TYPE OF ROSE, 'Arthur Bell' has many outstanding qualities: it is early flowering, withstands belting summer downpours, clearly presents its flowers on stiff stems, and has glossy leaves and good disease-resistance. It does need to be grown against a dark background though, because the yellow flowers end up being virtually cream-coloured. Prune in late winter, reducing the main stems to 25–45cm (10–18in) high, and cutting back sideshoots by about one-third of their length.

PLANT PROFILE	
HEIGHT 90cm (3ft)	
SPREAD 60cm (24in)	
TYPE Bush (cluster-flowered)	
HARDINESS Fully hardy	
FLOWERING Summer to autumn	

A AWAKENING ('Probuzini')

QUITE A STAR, with open, petal-packed flowers of the gentlest pink over summer and a sweet scent, AWAKENING was found growing in Czechoslovakia and introduced to northwest Europe in 1990. If you're looking for an alternative to the pink climber 'New Dawn' (*see page 201*), this is an excellent choice. Growth is not too rampant, making it ideal for arches and medium-high walls. Avoid pruning for the first couple of years, but train shoots horizontally. Once established, prune in the autumn, after flowering, nipping back the main stems if they are too long, and reducing sideshoots by two-thirds.

PLANT PROFILE

HEIGHT 3m (10ft)

TYPE Climber

HARDINESS Fully hardy

FLOWERING Summer to autumn

BABY MASQUERADE ('Tanba')

B

POPULAR FOR OVER 50 YEARS, and for very good reason, the flowers of BABY MASQUERADE change colour, starting off bright yellow before becoming flushed with a pinkish-red. Keep snipping off the fading blooms to encourage more and more. Growth is on the tall side for a miniature rose, and it forms a bushy plant with leathery leaves. Like other tall miniatures, it can be grown as edging, in pots, or right at the front of a border. In late winter remove all growth apart from the strongest shoots, and prune these back by one-third to one-half to force up plenty of new, vigorous, twiggy shoots.

PLANT PROFILE	
HEIGHT 40cm (16in)	
SPREAD 40cm (16in)	
TYPE Bush (miniature)	
HARDINESS Fully hardy	
FLOWERING Summer to autumn	

B | 'Ballerina'

A SUBTLE MIX OF CLEAR, LIGHT PINK COLOURING around the edge of each flower and the white colour within distinguishes the blooms of 'Ballerina'. The flowers are quite small at 3cm (1¼in) wide, but appear in massed sprays so that you can hardly see the leaves in midsummer when it is in full bloom. The scent is barely noticeable. Further flowers keep appearing all summer on the strong growth. 'Ballerina' can also be grown as a standard. To create a large shrub remove only diseased, dead, and damaged growth in late winter and give a light trim for shape. If you prune harder, fewer, larger flowers will result.

PLANT PROFILE

HEIGHT To 1.5m (5ft)

SPREAD 1.2m (4ft)

TYPE Shrub

HARDINESS Fully hardy

FLOWERING Summer to autumn

banksiae 'Lutea' Yellow banksian rose

B

A GOOD CHOICE FOR A STOUT TREE, this vigorous rose flowers in mid- to late spring and combines well with a summer-flowering clematis. The profusion of small, double yellow flowers on thornless stems makes a magnificent sight when shoots reach the crown of a tree, but a warm sheltered site is required because it is not totally hardy. In late summer, for the first two years only, prune sideshoots by 8cm (3in) to a strong new shoot. In the following years prune up to one-third of the oldest main stems back to ground level.

PLANT PROFILE	
HEIGHT To 6m (20ft)	
TYPE Rambler	
HARDINESS Frost hardy	
FLOWERING Mid- to late spring	

'Bantry Bay'

A FINE, MODEST CLIMBER FOR A WALL OR PILLAR, 'Bantry Bay' is always in flower over summer with rich pink blooms. Its free-branching habit means that it is liberally covered in colour, making it useful as a summer divide or as part of a hedge. It is remarkably healthy and will not get mildew even if grown against a wall. All it lacks is a rich, strong scent. Do not prune for the first two years, but train new shoots horizontally along their supports or around a pillar. From the third year prune in the autumn, after flowering, nipping back the main stems, and shortening sideshoots by two-thirds.

PLANT PROFILE

HEIGHT 4m (12ft)

TYPE Climber

HARDINESS Fully hardy

FLOWERING Summer to autumn

'Baron Girod de l'Ain'

B

A RATHER UNUSUAL ROSE, 'Baron Girod de l'Ain' is a Hybrid Perpetual with strong crimson flowers. Individual petals have a wavy outer edge coloured white. Put it at the front of a border where it can be easily seen (it is not too prickly) and you can get a whiff of its sweet scent. A must for lovers of old garden roses, it flowers prolifically over summer and has plenty of vigorous growth. In formal gardens prune shoots by one-half to two-thirds in late winter. In less formal and cottage gardens remove only diseased, dead, and damaged growth, and give a light overall prune for shape.

PLANT PROFILE

HEIGHT	1.2m (4ft)
SPREAD	90cm (3ft)
TYPE	Old garden rose
HARDINESS	Fully hardy
FLOWERING	Summer

B   'Belle de Crécy'

BELONGING TO PROBABLY THE OLDEST GROUP OF ROSES, the
Gallicas, 'Belle de Crécy' provides everything you could need.
There is one powerful burst of richly scented flowers in
midsummer, and their colour changes from cerise-pink on
opening to a softer hue (the colour change speeds up in hot
weather). Growth is on the lax, arching side, the stems have
few thorns, and the leaves are dark green. In late winter
remove diseased, dead, and damaged growth. If needed, prune
shoots for a balanced shape – harder pruning results in fewer
stems with larger flowers, and lighter pruning the reverse.

PLANT PROFILE

HEIGHT 1.2m (4ft)

SPREAD 90cm (3ft)

TYPE Old garden rose

HARDINESS Fully hardy

FLOWERING Midsummer

'Blairii Number Two'

B

DEEP PINK IN THE CENTRE, and pale pink around the outside, 'Blairii Number Two' is a climbing old garden rose, extremely popular for its large, petal-packed, scented flowers. Its one main flowering burst is well worth waiting for, and there may be a few sporadic flowers after that. Grow it up pillars and on walls or over pergolas, but do look out for the nasty prickles and mildew. The young leaves are reddish-green. In the first two years train new shoots into a horizontal position. Then start pruning in the autumn, after flowering, cutting back the main stems if necessary and reducing sideshoots by two-thirds.

PLANT PROFILE
HEIGHT 4m (12ft)
TYPE Climber
HARDINESS Fully hardy
FLOWERING Midsummer

B | 'Blanche Double de Coubert'

MAKING AN EXCELLENT SHRUB ROSE for the border, or an
open summer hedge or divide, 'Blanche Double de Coubert'
has scented white flowers (highlighted against the dark,
leathery foliage) in early summer. They keep appearing right
through the summer although the soft, papery petals suffer
after heavy rain. It has been extremely popular since being
introduced in France in 1892 and is often listed under Rugosa
roses in catalogues. Prune shoots in late winter by one-half to
two-thirds. Prune lightly for more flowering stems with
smaller blooms, and harder for fewer stems with larger flowers.

PLANT PROFILE

HEIGHT 1.5m (5ft)

SPREAD 1.2m (4ft)

TYPE Shrub

HARDINESS Fully hardy

FLOWERING Summer to autumn;
hips in late autumn

'Blessings'

B

A TOTALLY RELIABLE front-of-the-border rose, 'Blessings' keeps flowering all summer. The pink flowers (set against dark green leaves) withstand the rain and appear in such numbers that there are always plenty to spare for cutting, though they have minimal scent. They are an extremely useful choice in pastel colour schemes or where bolder colours need to be offset by a gentler tone. In late winter remove all unproductive stems, and prune the remaining ones to outward-facing buds 20–25cm (8–10in) above ground level. For large, showy flowers prune harder, leaving just two or three buds.

PLANT PROFILE	
HEIGHT	1.1m (3½ft)
SPREAD	75cm (30in)
TYPE	Bush (large-flowered)
HARDINESS	Fully hardy
FLOWERING	Summer to autumn

B | BLUE MOON ('Tannacht')

THE BEAUTIFUL FLOWERS OF BLUE MOON are high-pointed when in bud, and good for cutting. The name is misleading because the flowers are not in fact blue but closer to lavender, and they appear on long stems. If it is grown in dappled shade rather than bright sun, the colour will seem slightly darker. Growth is not too vigorous, and the leaves are dark green. In late winter remove all unproductive stems to ground level, and prune the rest hard to outward-facing buds 20–25cm (8–10in) above the soil. This helps keep the centre of the bush clear. For large, showy flowers prune harder to just two or three buds.

PLANT PROFILE	
HEIGHT	90cm (3ft)
SPREAD	70cm (28in)
TYPE	Bush (large-flowered)
HARDINESS	Fully hardy
FLOWERING	Summer to autumn

'Bobbie James'

B

IF YOU WANT A VIGOROUS, HIGH-POWERED RAMBLER to shoot into a tree, produce masses of clusters of buds, and then erupt in a great display of white flowers (once a summer), this is an excellent choice. Since being introduced in 1960 it has been a big favourite, not least for its healthy foliage and strong scent. Make sure that you give it plenty of room because this is not a rambler for a small, cramped space. For the first two years after planting prune sideshoots by 8cm (3in) to a strong, new shoot in late summer. Then prune up to one-third of the oldest stems back to ground level, leaving the new, productive ones.

PLANT PROFILE

HEIGHT To 10m (30ft)

TYPE Rambler

HARDINESS Fully hardy

FLOWERING Early summer

B | BONICA ('Meidomonac')

A FAILSAFE ROSE, BONICA is covered in pink flowers from low down, right the way up to the top of the bush, all through summer until the weather turns bad in the autumn. The large sprays of flowers are set against the rich green foliage. It can either be grown as a showstopper at the front of a border, or planted in a row to make a small divide across the garden. Sometimes called a ground-cover rose, it makes a shrubby mound with a spread greater than its height. Prune when dormant in winter, removing diseased, dead, and damaged growth. Trim lightly to help produce a balanced shape.

PLANT PROFILE

HEIGHT 85cm (34in)

SPREAD 1.1m (3½ft)

TYPE Shrub

HARDINESS Fully hardy

FLOWERING Summer to autumn

'Boule de Neige'

B

WORTH ITS PLACE IN A MIXED ROSE HEDGE, 'Boule de Neige' is a Bourbon rose that always makes an excellent show. The 8cm (3in) wide, scented flowers appear in clusters all summer long, while the leaves are glossy, dark green. The name, which translates as "snowball", describes the rounded white flowers but not the opening buds, which have an attractive red tint. In late winter prune shoots by one-half to two-thirds. Prune harder for fewer stems with larger flowers, and more lightly for more flowering stems with smaller blooms.

PLANT PROFILE	
HEIGHT	1.5m (5ft)
SPREAD	1.2m (4ft)
TYPE	Old garden rose
HARDINESS	Fully hardy
FLOWERING	Summer to autumn

B | 'Bourbon Queen'

A RICHLY SCENTED PINK, the flowers appear mainly in early summer on stems that can be quite vigorous, almost like those of a climber. If pruned to keep it shrubby, 'Bourbon Queen' has pleasantly wayward growth, making it just right for cottage gardens. The long stems have mid-green leaves. Introduced in 1835, this Bourbon rose will still be a big seller in 2035. To keep growth in check, prune stems in late winter by one-half to two-thirds. If you want fewer stems with larger flowers, prune hard; for more flowering stems with smaller blooms, remove less when pruning.

PLANT PROFILE

HEIGHT To 2.5m (8ft)

SPREAD 1.5m (5ft)

TYPE Old garden rose

HARDINESS Fully hardy

FLOWERING Summer

BREATH OF LIFE ('Harquanne')

B

WITH APRICOT FLOWERS THAT LAST WELL when cut, gradually taking on a pink tinge, BREATH OF LIFE is a modest climber. It can be grown up small walls or around pillars, but remember to gently bend down its stiff, upright young stems until they are horizontal so that they put out more flowering shoots low down, otherwise all the flowers will appear high up and out of reach. Leave it unpruned for the first two years, then prune in the autumn, after flowering, nipping back the main stems if necessary and shortening sideshoots by two-thirds.

PLANT PROFILE

HEIGHT 2.5m (8ft)

TYPE Climber

HARDINESS Fully hardy

FLOWERING Summer to autumn

B BRIGHT SMILE ('Dicdance')

NEAT, BUSHY, AND LOW GROWING (in fact, so low that some catalogues list it as a patio rose), BRIGHT SMILE offers large, open flowers and tight, slender buds, which keep emerging through the growing season. It is a summery mix of bright yellow, gently scented flowers and glossy, bright green leaves. Small, high-value roses like this are well worth a place in most gardens, either at the front of a border or to edge paths. Prune in late winter, removing all growth apart from the strongest shoots. Cut these back by one-third to one-half to force up plenty of new, vigorous growth.

PLANT PROFILE

HEIGHT 45cm (18in)

SPREAD 45cm (18in)

TYPE Bush (cluster-flowered, miniature)

HARDINESS Fully hardy

FLOWERING Summer to autumn

BROADLANDS ('Tanmirson')

BROAD IS AN APPROPRIATE DESCRIPTION for this wide-spreading, low-growing, healthy rose, which keeps flowering over summer. The scented flowers are flashy yellow, and the leaves light green. Growth is vigorous, and though it is not so dense and tangled as to keep down and suppress weeds, it will create a flowery background for ponds, adding shade for the frogs and toads. Minimal pruning is required, but if growth is getting too rampant, cut it back to an outward-facing bud in late winter. Shorten sideshoots at the same time if necessary.

B

PLANT PROFILE

HEIGHT 50cm (20in)

SPREAD 1.5m (5ft)

TYPE Ground-cover

HARDINESS Fully hardy

FLOWERING Summer

B

'Buff Beauty'

AN EXCELLENT, BUSHY SHRUB, 'Buff Beauty' adds plenty of impact when grown against a wall or fence, and it can also be grown as a standard. It has sweet-scented, marmalade or apricot flowers that gently fade, and dark, glossy leaves, adding a muted contrast to the colour scheme. The young stems are an attractive reddish-brown. The main burst of flowers (in large trusses) is in midsummer, with more following. Prune in late winter to remove diseased, dead, and damaged growth, leaving the old wood intact. If you need to create a more balanced shape, trim the remaining shoots.

PLANT PROFILE

HEIGHT 1.2m (4ft)

SPREAD 1.2m (4ft)

TYPE Shrub

HARDINESS Fully hardy

FLOWERING Summer

'Camaïeux'

C

THIS EXTRAORDINARY GALLICA ROSE has striped, scented flowers, which appear in one burst in midsummer. They are reddish-pink, turning a lavender-lilac purple, splashed or striped with white. It might sound a touch brash but the effect is surprisingly subtle. Though the plant is on the short side, growth is vigorous. Use it among a collection of old garden roses. To prune, remove diseased, dead, and damaged growth in late winter. Cut back lightly to give a balanced shape with many stems and smaller blooms, or prune harder for fewer stems with larger flowers.

PLANT PROFILE

HEIGHT	80cm (32in)
SPREAD	80cm (32in)
TYPE	Old garden rose
HARDINESS	Fully hardy
FLOWERING	Midsummer

C | *canina* Dog rose

ONE FOR THE WILD OR COTTAGE GARDEN, the dog rose is often seen in wild hedgerows where its stems make plenty of dense, tangled growth. It is best known for its show of red hips, which are full of Vitamin C and are used to make rose-hip syrup. The dog rose is not necessarily the best rose for hedges as it is not particularly showy, but it is of value to wildlife, and its thorny growth should deter most intruders, animal and human. It is hard to prune due to its dense habit; remove only diseased, dead, and damaged growth, and trim overlong shoots to create a balanced shape.

PLANT PROFILE

HEIGHT To 3m (10ft)

SPREAD 2m (6ft)

TYPE Wild

HARDINESS Fully hardy

FLOWERING Summer; hips in autumn

'Cantabrigiensis'

C

MAKING ITS FIRST APPEARANCE in Cambridge Botanic Garden in the 1930s, 'Cantabrigiensis' makes vigorous, shrubby growth, with pale yellow flowers opening right at the end of spring for a few weeks. It is a marvellous sight, at its best in cottage or wildflower gardens. It also provides a colourful link between the main burst of spring-flowering plants and those opening at the start of the summer season. Keep pruning to a minimum, removing only diseased, dead, and damaged growth, and trimming unruly shoots in late winter for a balanced shape.

PLANT PROFILE

HEIGHT 2.5m (8ft)

SPREAD 2.5m (8ft)

TYPE Shrub

HARDINESS Fully hardy

FLOWERING Late spring and early summer; hips in autumn

C | 'Cardinal de Richelieu'

AMONG THE VERY BEST of the old Gallica roses, 'Cardinal de Richelieu' has one superb flush of flowers before midsummer. The blooms are richly coloured (dark to royal purple) with a sweet scent, set against dark green leaves. Even the round buds are attractive. There are few thorns, and the overall shape is on the neat and tidy side. Give it a prominent place where you can smell the flowers. To create an impressive shrub remove only diseased, dead, and damaged growth, and leave the old wood intact. In late winter trim long shoots to give a balanced shape. Harder pruning gives fewer stems with larger flowers.

PLANT PROFILE

HEIGHT 90cm (3ft)

SPREAD 1.2m (4ft)

TYPE Old garden rose

HARDINESS Fully hardy

FLOWERING Summer

CASINO ('Macca')

A FIRST-RATE CLIMBER, with soft-yellow, gently scented flowers that emerge from pointed buds and slowly fade. At 3m (10ft) high, it does not get out of hand, and is an excellent choice for a trellis, pergola, or small wall. The dark green leaves are slightly sparse. It dislikes cold, exposed areas, and is therefore best in a sunny, protected site. As new shoots develop over the first two years, train them horizontally to produce flowering sideshoots. Once the shape of the plant is established, prune in the autumn after flowering, trimming the main stems as needed, and reducing sideshoots by two-thirds.

PLANT PROFILE	
HEIGHT 3m (10ft)	
TYPE Climber	
HARDINESS Fully hardy	
FLOWERING Summer to autumn	

C | 'Cécile Brünner'

SMALL, TWIGGY, AND PRETTY are the best words to describe this China rose. Large clusters of petite, beautiful flowers open from pointed, shapely buds. The growth is twiggy, and the show of dark green leaves is on the sparse side. The overall shape has a light, neat touch, making it excellent for small courtyards or tubs where nothing too chunky is required. It is a popular plant for the almost-constant show of flowers through the growing season. Prune it in late winter, cutting shoots by one-half to two-thirds. Pruning by two-thirds will give fewer stems with larger flowers.

PLANT PROFILE	
HEIGHT 75cm (30in)	
SPREAD 60cm (24in)	
TYPE Old garden rose	
HARDINESS Fully hardy	
FLOWERING Summer to autumn	

'Céleste'

C

'CÉLESTE' IS HIGHLY VALUED for its attractive, dark pink buds, which open to reveal shell-pink, scented flowers with yellow stamens. The lightness of tone blends well with the grey-green leaves. It is sometimes listed in catalogues as 'Celestial', where it usually appears with the Alba roses. It tolerates less-than-ideal growing conditions and can be grown as a hedge. To maintain it as a large shrub remove only diseased, dead, and damaged growth. A minimal late winter prune gives a balanced shape. For fewer but larger flowers, prune harder, otherwise it will produce more stems with smaller blooms.

PLANT PROFILE

HEIGHT	1.5m (5ft)
SPREAD	1.2m (4ft)
TYPE	Old garden rose
HARDINESS	Fully hardy
FLOWERING	Midsummer

C | x *centifolia* 'Cristata' Crested moss rose

SOME ROSES ARE GROWN more for their neat, tidy growth, and some for their excellent flowers; this Moss rose is definitely one of the latter. The shape is lax and open, and some gardeners stake the stems to stop them bending right down, though that is not a problem in easy-going cottage gardens. The branching, arching stems are covered in rose-pink flowers, and the opening buds are equally stunning. To create and maintain the naturally striking, lax bush shape remove only diseased, dead, and damaged growth in winter, and leave the old wood intact. Little other pruning is required.

PLANT PROFILE	
HEIGHT 1.5m (5ft)	
SPREAD 1.2m (4ft)	
TYPE Old garden rose	
HARDINESS Fully hardy	
FLOWERING Summer	

x *centifolia* 'Muscosa' Common moss rose

C

INTERESTING MOSSY GROWTH on the lax, prickly stems and just below the attractive, deep pink flowers makes *Rosa* x *centifolia* 'Muscosa' appealing to plant collectors, among others. Like the similar *R.* x *centifolia* 'Cristata' (*see facing page*), it is generally listed in rose catalogues with the group called Moss roses, which were a big hit in Victorian times. Minimal pruning is needed: remove only diseased, dead, and damaged growth to obtain a large, impressive shrub. If you need to trim shoots for a balanced shape, do this in late winter.

PLANT PROFILE

HEIGHT 1.5m (5ft)

SPREAD 1.2m (4ft)

TYPE Old garden rose

HARDINESS Fully hardy

FLOWERING Summer

C | 'Cerise Bouquet'

A MASSIVE SHRUB ROSE, 'Cerise Bouquet' has enormous presence in the border or as a feature in its own bed in a large lawn. It can also be used in a hedge of mixed roses. Growth is strong and arching, the leaves are grey-green, and the clusters of 6cm (2½in) wide flowers are lipstick-red. There is sometimes a second crop of flowers towards the end of summer. Prune in late winter. If you would like fewer, larger flowers, prune hard. Otherwise, prune lightly, removing diseased, dead, and damaged growth, and leaving the old wood intact; select overlong shoots to trim for a balanced shape.

PLANT PROFILE

HEIGHT To 3.5m (11ft)

SPREAD To 3.5m (11ft)

TYPE Shrub

HARDINESS Fully hardy

FLOWERING Summer

'Charles de Mills'

ONE OF THE BEST-LOVED GALLICA ROSES, 'Charles de Mills'
is popular for two reasons: it has large, lightly scented, petal-
packed flowers, about 10cm (4in) wide, which have an
incredibly flat surface; and the colour is rich, dark red with
hints of lilac and purple. Growth is vigorous, sometimes even
arching, and the lack of prickles makes it good for the front
of a border. For a large shrub, remove only diseased, dead, and
damaged growth. An additional light, late-winter prune gives
a balanced shape and encourages more stems with smaller
blooms. Harder pruning gives fewer stems with larger flowers.

C

PLANT PROFILE	
HEIGHT 1.2m (4ft)	
SPREAD 1.2m (4ft)	
TYPE Old garden rose	
HARDINESS Fully hardy	
FLOWERING Midsummer	

C | 'Chinatown'

THE WELL-SCENTED, YELLOW FLOWERS have a slight pink tinge, and they cover the stems through most of the summer, making a vigorous show and even withstanding bad weather. The attractive background leaf colour is glossy, dark green. Tough and reliable, 'Chinatown' can be used to keep borders alive and colourful, or be incorporated as part of a medium-high mixed hedge. It is a top choice that will not let you down. In late winter cut back the main stems to 25–45cm (10–18in) above ground level, and reduce sideshoots by about two-thirds of their length.

PLANT PROFILE

HEIGHT	1.2m (4ft)
SPREAD	90cm (3ft)
TYPE	Bush (cluster-flowered)
HARDINESS	Fully hardy
FLOWERING	Summer to autumn

CIDER CUP ('Dicladida')

C

ONE OF THE BEST of the more recent patio roses, CIDER CUP has everything you could want except a strong, rich scent. With a small, neat, bushy shape, attractive, high-pointed buds, and a long show of attractive, marmalade-yellow flowers (also good for cutting), it withstands summer rain and still looks good. It is equally effective in pots or when used as an edging plant, or in semi-circles in front of a garden statue. Prune to encourage plenty of new, vigorous growth. In late winter remove all growth apart from the strongest shoots, and then cut them back by one-third to one-half.

PLANT PROFILE	
HEIGHT 45cm (18in)	
SPREAD 45cm (18in)	
TYPE Bush (cluster-flowered, patio)	
HARDINESS Fully hardy	
FLOWERING Summer	

C | CITY OF LONDON ('Harukfore')

THE BEAUTIFULLY SHAPED FLOWERS, soft pink and highly scented, gradually fade in colour, and make a gentle addition to pastel borders. Growth is vigorous, clusters of small flowers keep appearing, and the background leaf colour is healthy, glossy green. CITY OF LONDON has been deservedly popular since its introduction in 1988. For a reasonably compact bush, in late winter cut back the main stems to 25–45cm (10–18in) above the ground, and reduce sideshoots by about one-third. If you do not follow the pruning regime, CITY OF LONDON will grow much taller, reaching 1.5m (5ft) or possibly even higher.

PLANT PROFILE

HEIGHT	80cm (32in)
SPREAD	75cm (30in)
TYPE	Bush (cluster-flowered)
HARDINESS	Fully hardy
FLOWERING	Summer to autumn

'Climbing Etoile de Hollande'

C

A WONDERFUL CLIMBER, this has lax, arching stems and enormous, richly scented flowers. The large buds start opening in early summer when it has its main burst of blooms. The crimson flowers have a lovely, sweet scent and, being 13cm (5in) wide, tend to hang down, especially after heavy rain, which adds to the sense of opulence. After the first flush of flowers, more will appear. Avoid pruning for the first two years, but train new shoots into a horizontal position. In the following years prune in the autumn, nipping back the main stems as needed and shortening sideshoots by two-thirds.

PLANT PROFILE

HEIGHT 6m (20ft)

TYPE Climber

HARDINESS Fully hardy

FLOWERING Summer

C | 'Climbing Lady Hillingdon'

WHILE IT PERFORMS WELL in poor conditions, 'Climbing Lady Hillingdon' is invariably best grown against a hot, sunny wall where its arching stems produce 8cm (3in) wide flowers that are open and apricot-yellow, with a strong, sweet scent. The new stems are a beautiful red, though it can take a few years for the basic framework to start sending them out. A main burst of flowers in early summer is followed by more. Avoid pruning for the first two years, training new shoots into a horizontal position. Then prune after flowering, cutting back the main stems if necessary and sideshoots by two-thirds.

PLANT PROFILE

HEIGHT To 5m (15ft)

TYPE Climber

HARDINESS Fully hardy

FLOWERING Summer to autumn

'Climbing Mrs Sam McGredy'

C

THIS HIGHLY REGARDED CLIMBING VERSION of a large-flowered bush has copper-orange flowers, which sets it apart from the mass of red, pink, and white climbers. The leaves have a bronze tint, the buds are reddish-brown, and the flowers are initially high-pointed before they open and flatten out. The display keeps going reliably until autumn. In the first two years simply train new shoots into a horizontal position to encourage plenty of flowering sideshoots. In the following years prune in the autumn, after flowering, nipping back the main stems as needed and shortening sideshoots by two-thirds.

PLANT PROFILE	
HEIGHT	5m (15ft)
TYPE	Climber
HARDINESS	Fully hardy
FLOWERING	Summer to autumn

C

'Compassion'

A HIGH-QUALITY CLIMBER, 'Compassion' has picked up many awards since being introduced in 1973 because it has all the key ingredients of a successful rose. It has superb scent, beautiful colours, with a touch of apricot to add to the soft pink, and a constant supply of shapely flowers all summer. Modestly rampant, it is ideal for a small wall or pillar, with a covering of glossy leaves. It exudes good health. Avoid pruning for the first two years, but train new shoots into a horizontal position. Once established, prune in the autumn, nipping back the main stems, and shortening sideshoots by two-thirds.

PLANT PROFILE

HEIGHT 3m (10ft)

TYPE Climber

HARDINESS Fully hardy

FLOWERING Summer to autumn

'Complicata'

C

A SUPERB, BUSHY GALLICA ROSE, 'Complicata' has very large, 10cm (4in) wide flowers with a gentle scent. What makes them so eye-catching is the white base of the petals and the yellow stamens. Tough and robust, it can be grown as an early-summer-flowering hedge or in a garden of old roses, but allow space for its arching stems. To create a large shrub remove diseased, dead, and damaged growth in late winter, and leave the old wood. Give a minimal trim for a balanced shape and plenty of stems with smaller blooms. If you prune harder it will produce fewer stems with larger flowers.

PLANT PROFILE	
HEIGHT	2.2m (7ft)
SPREAD	2.5m (8ft)
TYPE	Old garden rose
HARDINESS	Fully hardy
FLOWERING	Midsummer

C | CONGRATULATIONS ('Korlift')

WITH ITS POINTED BUDS, plenty of flowers (good for cutting) all summer, and dark green leaves, CONGRATULATIONS is a useful addition to a mixed border. It is nearly twice as tall as it is wide, which needs thinking about when positioning it. An alternative is to plant it in rows to make a summer hedge or divide; being quite narrow, it does not take up too much room. When pruning you are aiming for an open-centred bush. In late winter remove all unproductive stems, and prune hard to outward-facing buds 20–25cm (8–10in) above ground level. For larger flowers prune harder, to two or three buds.

PLANT PROFILE	
HEIGHT	1.5m (5ft)
SPREAD	90cm (3ft)
TYPE	Bush (large-flowered)
HARDINESS	Fully hardy
FLOWERING	Summer to autumn

'Conrad Ferdinand Meyer'

C

A SUPERB ROSE for the back of the border, where its arching, thorny stems bear large, 10cm (4in) wide, wonderfully scented flowers. The grey-green leaves are also large. There are usually two flowering bursts, one in early summer and one in early autumn, with the latter being better than the first. Growth is vigorous. To create a large shrub remove only diseased, dead, and damaged growth, and leave the old wood. A light prune in late winter also helps to give a balanced shape and more flowering stems with smaller blooms. Harder pruning gives fewer stems with larger flowers.

PLANT PROFILE	
HEIGHT	2.5m (8ft)
SPREAD	2m (6ft)
TYPE	Shrub
HARDINESS	Fully hardy
FLOWERING	Summer and autumn

C | CONSERVATION ('Cocdimple')

INTRODUCED TO MARK THE 50TH ANNIVERSARY of the World Wildlife Fund, CONSERVATION is a short, compact, bushy, mounding plant that flowers right through the summer. The apricot-pink blooms are nicely set off by the glossy leaves. A high-performance patio rose, highlight it in a pot or grow it in gaps where stones have been removed in a large terrace. Prune to keep a good supply of new, vigorous, twiggy growth. In late winter remove all but the strongest shoots, and then cut them back by one-third to one-half.

PLANT PROFILE

HEIGHT	45cm (18in)
SPREAD	45cm (18in)
TYPE	Bush (cluster-flowered, patio)
HARDINESS	Fully hardy
FLOWERING	Summer to autumn

CONSTANCE SPRY ('Austance')

C

A DUAL-PURPOSE ROSE, CONSTANCE SPRY can be grown as a rampant shrub at the back of a border, or as a moderate climber against a wall where it will hit 3m (10ft) or more (some catalogues actually list it as a climber). The 13cm (5in) wide flowers have a strong scent, and are borne on thorny stems. Although they appear only once, they make a spectacular show. The foliage hangs on over winter, and often needs spraying against mildew in summer. When pruning, remove diseased, dead, and damaged growth, and leave the old wood intact. Cut back lightly to promote a balanced shape.

PLANT PROFILE

HEIGHT 2m (6ft) as a shrub; 3m (10ft) as a climber

SPREAD 1.5m (5ft) as a shrub

TYPE Shrub and climber

HARDINESS Fully hardy

FLOWERING Midsummer

C | 'Cornelia'

IT IS RARE TO GROW A ROSE for its autumn show of flowers, but the best sprays of 'Cornelia', bigger and more richly coloured, open just after the end of summer. The first blooms open in early summer and are apricot, fading to pink, against dark green leaves. Its substantial size means it makes an effective hedge, especially where it catches the autumn sun on the copper-red buds. Little pruning is needed: remove only diseased, dead, and damaged growth, and trim overlong shoots in late winter. This minimal regime encourages many small blooms; harder pruning will result in larger flowers.

PLANT PROFILE

HEIGHT	1.5m (5ft)
SPREAD	1.5m (5ft)
TYPE	Shrub
HARDINESS	Fully hardy
FLOWERING	Summer to autumn

'Crimson Glory'

C

AN EXQUISITE, SMALL, CRIMSON ROSE, this has beautifully
shaped, velvety flowers with a fabulous scent. They give a long
display right through the growing season on bushy growth
with dark green leaves. The leaves are prone to mildew and
the stems are prickly, but that is no reason to be put off. If you
have a gap at the front of a border, or want roses for your
buttonhole, grow it. For a healthy, open-centred bush remove
all unproductive stems in late winter, and prune the remaining
ones to outward-facing buds 20–25cm (8–10in) above ground
level. For large, showy flowers prune to just two or three buds.

PLANT PROFILE	
HEIGHT 60cm (24in)	
SPREAD 60cm (24in)	
TYPE Bush (large-flowered)	
HARDINESS Fully hardy	
FLOWERING Summer to autumn	

C | 'Crimson Shower'

MOST RAMBLERS TEND TO FLOWER only once in midsummer, but 'Crimson Shower' has a surprisingly long flowering period, starting soon after midsummer and continuing until the beginning of autumn. Train the stems into trees or around pillars or pergolas, where the bright red flowers add plenty of colour. For the first two years prune sideshoots by 8cm (3in) to a strong, new shoot. In the following years prune at most one-third of the oldest main stems back to ground level. It can also be grown as a very effective weeping standard.

PLANT PROFILE

HEIGHT 5m (15ft)

TYPE Rambler

HARDINESS Fully hardy

FLOWERING Summer to autumn

x *damascena* var. *semperflorens* Autumn damask rose

D

ALSO KNOWN AS THE FOUR SEASONS ROSE, this Damask rose has a highly impressive ability to keep flowering from early summer (its main burst) to mid-autumn (more in sporadic bursts) The leaves are, unusually, light green, and the attractive, scented flowers, which are quite large at nearly 10cm (4in) wide on the arching stems, are clear rose-pink. In late winter prune by one-half to two-thirds. Prune harder for fewer stems with larger flowers, and more lightly for more stems with smaller blooms.

PLANT PROFILE
HEIGHT 1.5m (5ft)
SPREAD 1.2m (4ft)
TYPE Old garden rose
HARDINESS Fully hardy
FLOWERING Early summer to mid-autumn

D | 'Danse du Feu'

A GOOD CLIMBER FOR A COLD, SHADY WALL, 'Danse du Feu' is
at its most attractive when in bud with many flowers half-
open. The blooms have a neat, tight shape and strong colour.
As the petals open and lengthen, the colour starts to fade to
orange-red, but the repeat-flowering does provide good colour
against white walls. Avoid pruning for the first two years, but
train new shoots horizontally to produce flowering sideshoots.
From the third year prune in the autumn, after flowering,
nipping back the main stems if necessary and shortening
sideshoots by two-thirds.

PLANT PROFILE

HEIGHT 2.5m (8ft)

TYPE Climber

HARDINESS Fully hardy

FLOWERING Summer to autumn

DAWN CHORUS ('Dicquasar')

D

CLASSIC, HIGH-POINTED BUDS open to marmalade-orange flowers with a hint of yellow. The very lightly scented flowers are quite prolific, appearing through summer into the start of autumn. DAWN CHORUS holds its own in hot colour schemes, and can be used with the likes of subtropical cannas. It can also be grown in a more traditional way, as a standard. In late winter remove all unproductive stems, and prune hard to outward-facing buds 20–25cm (8–10in) above the ground. This helps deter crisscrossing shoots in the centre. For large, showy flowers, prune harder, leaving just two or three buds.

PLANT PROFILE	
HEIGHT	90cm (3ft)
SPREAD	75cm (30in)
TYPE	Bush (large-flowered)
HARDINESS	Fully hardy
FLOWERING	Summer to autumn

D 'Deep Secret'

ONE OF THE VERY BEST large-flowered bush roses, 'Deep Secret' has exquisitely shapely buds and flowers, a deep, rich red colour (even darker in the case of the buds), a sweet scent, glossy green leaves, and bushy growth. It is well worth including in any display of roses, makes a very classy standard, and is excellent for cut flowers. Remove unproductive stems in late winter, and prune hard to outward-facing buds 20–25cm (8–10in) from the soil. For large, showy flowers prune harder, leaving just two or three buds. Cutting to outward-facing buds keeps the centre of the bush clear.

PLANT PROFILE

HEIGHT 90m (3ft)

SPREAD 75cm (30in)

TYPE Bush (large-flowered)

HARDINESS Fully hardy

FLOWERING Summer to autumn

'Desprez à Fleurs Jaunes'

D

EXCELLENT IN COTTAGE GARDENS, 'Desprez à Fleurs Jaunes'
has lax, arching stems and, in early summer, the tight pinkish-
white buds open to reveal flat-surfaced flowers. They are white
from a distance, but up-close the colour is more creamy-white
with a gentle tinge of pink and yellow to the petal edges. The
scent is of tangy, fresh-cut apples. No pruning is needed for
the first two years, but train new shoots horizontally. Then
prune in the autumn, after flowering, trimming the main
stems if they are too long, and sideshoots by two-thirds.

PLANT PROFILE	
HEIGHT 5m (15ft)	
TYPE Climber	
HARDINESS Frost hardy	
FLOWERING Summer	

D | 'Doris Tysterman'

OFTEN USED IN BOLD, BRIGHT COLOUR SCHEMES, 'Doris Tysterman' has a long summer show of orange-red flowers with darker hues at the edge of the petals. The growth stands smartly upright, holding up the flowers well against the glossy, dark green leaves. It is sometimes prone to mildew. In late winter remove any unproductive stems, and prune the remainder hard to outward-facing buds at 20–25cm (8–10in) along the stem. This helps remove crisscrossing shoots in the centre. For large, showy flowers prune harder, leaving just two or three buds.

PLANT PROFILE

HEIGHT 1.2m (4ft)

SPREAD 75cm (30in)

TYPE Bush (large-flowered)

HARDINESS Fully hardy

FLOWERING Summer to autumn

'Dorothy Perkins'

D

FLOWERING AFTER MOST RAMBLERS HAVE FINISHED, in the second half of summer, 'Dorothy Perkins' is a valuable addition to the garden although it does suffer from mildew. It provides a lavish show of plump, rose-pink flowers with quilled petals against a background of dark green leaves. Either send the stems up and round a pillar or pergola, or into a tree, or grow them against a wall. In late summer, for the first two years, prune sideshoots by 8cm (3in) to a strong, new shoot. In subsequent years prune up to one-third of the oldest main stems back to ground level.

PLANT PROFILE

HEIGHT 3m (10ft)

TYPE Rambler

HARDINESS Fully hardy

FLOWERING Late summer

D | 'Dortmund'

A PROLIFIC CLIMBER that never gets out of hand, 'Dortmund' immediately stands out with its five-petalled, red flowers with a white eye and yellow-orange stamens in the centre. It makes an excellent choice for pergolas and pillars, not least for its healthy, glossy green foliage and long show of flowers. All it lacks is scent. Avoid pruning for the first two years, simply training new shoots into a horizontal position to produce flowering sideshoots. From the third year prune in the autumn, after flowering, trimming back the main stems if they outgrow the space and reducing sideshoots by two-thirds.

PLANT PROFILE

HEIGHT 3m (10ft)

TYPE Climber

HARDINESS Fully hardy

FLOWERING Summer to autumn

'Du Maître d'Ecole'

D

A SUPERB OLD GALLICA ROSE, dating from 1840, 'Du Maître d'Ecole' is grown for its large, 10cm (4in) wide, heavy flowers, which are even larger on rich soils. The colour begins rose-pink, then gradually changes to lilac-pink with a green dot in the centre. The flowers are well spaced on the upright, almost thorn-free growth that has dark green leaves. Some catalogues call this rose 'De la Maître d'Ecole'. To prune, remove only diseased, dead, and damaged growth, and leave the old wood. A minimal late-winter prune also gives a balanced shape, with harder pruning producing fewer stems with larger flowers.

PLANT PROFILE	
HEIGHT	1.2m (4ft)
SPREAD	1.2m (4ft)
TYPE	Old garden rose
HARDINESS	Fully hardy
FLOWERING	Midsummer

D | DUBLIN BAY ('Macdub')

AN EXCELLENT RED CLIMBER, DUBLIN BAY has everything you could want in a rose except a satisfying, rich scent. The buds and flowers are shapely (because they belong to the large-flowered group of roses), the colour is strong, vivid red, the clusters of blooms give a constant display, and the healthy, glossy foliage completes the package. Avoid pruning for the first two years, but train new shoots into a horizontal position. Then prune in the autumn, nipping back the main stems if they are too long, and cutting back sideshoots by two-thirds. With harder pruning it can also form a shrub.

PLANT PROFILE

HEIGHT 2.2m (7ft)

TYPE Climber

HARDINESS Fully hardy

FLOWERING Summer to autumn

'Duc de Guiche'

D

ONE OF THE BEST GALLICAS, this should be in every collection of old garden roses. The buds appear in clusters, the 10cm (4in) wide flowers are richly coloured with a hint of lilac and a tiny green eye in the centre, the scent is deep, and the dense growth gently arching and sprawling. It flowers only once in midsummer, but the display is worth waiting for. Remove only diseased, dead, and damaged growth for an impressive shrub, and leave the old wood intact. A minimal late-winter prune also helps produce a balanced shape. If you prune harder, fewer stems with larger flowers will be produced.

PLANT PROFILE	
HEIGHT 1.2m (4ft)	
SPREAD 1.2m (4ft)	
TYPE Old garden rose	
HARDINESS Fully hardy	
FLOWERING Summer	

D | 'Dupontii' Snowbush rose

AT 2.2M (7FT) HIGH, 'Dupontii' makes a large, shrubby plant that can be grown against a wall, as a border background, or in rows to create a substantial hedge. In fact, the nearer you can get to smell the flowers the better because they have the fruity aroma of bubblegum and bananas. The nearly thornless stems tend to arch, and have grey-green leaves. The flowers are followed by orange autumn hips. Remove diseased, dead, and damaged growth and, in late winter, prune lightly to produce a balanced shape and plenty of stems with small blooms. If you prune harder the rose will produce fewer but larger flowers.

PLANT PROFILE

HEIGHT 2.2m (7ft)

SPREAD 2.2m (7ft)

TYPE Shrub

HARDINESS Fully hardy

FLOWERING Midsummer; hips in autumn

'Dutch Gold'

D

THE SCENTED FLOWERS OF 'DUTCH GOLD' are large (good for cutting) and can reach 15cm (6in) wide; the bright yellow colour does not fade, and the flowers withstand bad weather and rain. It is well covered in large, glossy, dark green leaves and is a good choice for the front of a border. It might be small, but it is a vigorous bush rose. Remove all unproductive stems in late winter, and prune hard to outward-facing buds at 20–25cm (8–10in). For large, showy flowers prune harder, leaving just two or three buds.

PLANT PROFILE	
HEIGHT	1.1m (3½ft)
SPREAD	75cm (30in)
TYPE	Bush (large-flowered)
HARDINESS	Fully hardy
FLOWERING	Summer to autumn

E | EGLANTYNE ('Ausmak')

THE PALE PINK FLOWERS have the rich scent of an old garden rose and keep flowering for a long period over summer. The growth is modest, twiggy, and bushy, with attractive green leaves, and is ideally suited to pastel schemes with mixed planting. EGLANTYNE also makes a graceful show when set in rows to edge a path. The cut flowers last for a long time in water. Prune shoots by one-half to two-thirds in late winter. The harder you prune the fewer the resulting stems and the larger the flowers.

PLANT PROFILE

HEIGHT 1.1m (3½ft)

SPREAD 90cm (3ft)

TYPE Shrub

HARDINESS Fully hardy

FLOWERING Summer

ELINA ('Dicjana')

E

STILL KNOWN TO SOME AS 'PEAUDOUCE', this rose has a handful of top awards. It is a beauty in the garden and worth growing because of its large flowers (virtually scentless) up to 15cm (6in) wide, which withstand the summer rain. They are nicely highlighted against the disease-resistant, glossy, dark green leaves. Even the fattening buds look stylish. Prune in late winter, removing all unproductive stems, and cutting to outward-facing buds, leaving 20–25cm (8–10in) of stem above ground. This helps discourage crossing shoots in the centre. For larger, more showy flowers prune to two or three buds.

PLANT PROFILE	
HEIGHT	1.1m (3½ft)
SPREAD	75cm (30in)
TYPE	Bush (large-flowered)
HARDINESS	Fully hardy
FLOWERING	Summer to autumn

E | 'Elizabeth Harkness'

EXPERTS WAX LYRICAL ABOUT THIS ROSE, calling it "refined". The flowers are creamy-white, tinged with rose-pink, and are attractively shaped, with the first opening in early summer and the display continuing until autumn, against dark green leaves. Put your nose right in to get a whiff of the sweet scent. It makes a good choice for borders and rose schemes, as well as cut-flower arrangements. When pruning you are aiming for an open-centred bush. In late winter remove all unproductive stems, and cut the rest to outward-facing buds at 20–25cm (8–10in). For large, showy flowers prune to two or three buds.

PLANT PROFILE

HEIGHT 80cm (32in)

SPREAD 60cm (24in)

TYPE Bush (large-flowered)

HARDINESS Fully hardy

FLOWERING Summer to autumn

'Emily Gray'

E

IF YOU WANT BUFF-YELLOW or yellowish-marmalade flowers, this is the rambler to chose. The scented flowers are not as prolific as on some ramblers but you will still have a very good display, and the stems put on plenty of growth. Most of the leaves hang on all year, especially in mild regions and, when the new spring foliage appears, it turns from attractive copper-red to glossy dark green. In late summer, for the first couple of years, prune sideshoots by 8cm (3in) to a strong, new shoot. In the following years, prune at most one-third of the oldest main stems back to ground level.

PLANT PROFILE

HEIGHT To 5m (15ft)

TYPE Rambler

HARDINESS Fully hardy

FLOWERING Midsummer

E

'Empereur du Maroc'

RICHLY, EXQUISITELY SCENTED FLOWERS have 40 or so petals with a deep, dark red colour, making it one of the darkest of its kind. This high-quality 19th-century Hybrid Perpetual rose is free-flowering over summer, more than making up for its slight tendency to mildew, the prickles, and the fact that it needs plenty of manure to fuel its flowers. In formal gardens prune shoots by one-half to two-thirds in late winter. In less formal and cottage gardens remove only diseased, dead, and damaged growth, and give a light overall prune for shape.

PLANT PROFILE	
HEIGHT	1.2m (4ft)
SPREAD	90cm (3ft)
TYPE	Old garden rose
HARDINESS	Fully hardy
FLOWERING	Summer

'Ena Harkness'

E

A BIG HIT IN THE 1950s, when gardeners could not get enough of its strong-coloured, scented flowers, 'Ena Harkness' was a firm favourite at the front of borders, especially for end-of-season colour. There followed a backlash when other roses became more popular thanks to their fuller covering of leaves and stronger flower stalks, but it remains a very good rose. The related 'Climbing Ena Harkness' grows to 5m (15ft). Remove all unproductive stems in late winter, and prune the remainder hard to outward-facing buds at 20–25cm (8–10in). For large, showy flowers prune harder, leaving just two or three buds.

PLANT PROFILE	
HEIGHT	75cm (30in)
SPREAD	60cm (24in)
TYPE	Bush (large-flowered)
HARDINESS	Fully hardy
FLOWERING	Summer to autumn

E | ENGLISH GARDEN ('Ausbuff')

MIXING OLD GARDEN ROSE TYPE FLOWERS and a modern tendency to repeat-flowering, ENGLISH GARDEN (introduced in 1986) has slightly scented flowers, apricot to buff-yellow in the centre, turning paler towards the edge of the petals. It is good at extending pastel colour schemes. ENGLISH GARDEN is taller than it is wide, and is a good candidate for sandwiching in gaps in a border or rose bed. In late winter prune stems by one-half to two-thirds. Harder pruning will result in fewer stems with larger flowers, and lighter pruning more flowering stems with smaller blooms.

PLANT PROFILE

HEIGHT 90cm (3ft)

SPREAD 75cm (30in)

TYPE Shrub

HARDINESS Fully hardy

FLOWERING Summer to autumn

'English Miss'

THE NICELY SCENTED FLOWERS have the soft, pale colour of a pinkish face and are set against a mass of leathery, dark green leaves. Look closely and you will see that the blooms, which appear all summer long, held in clusters, are packed with up to 60 petals. This is a quiet and gentle beauty with a highly appropriate name. Its small, compact shape makes it a good choice for the front of a bedding scheme or border. In late winter cut back main stems to 25–45cm (10–18in), and trim the sideshoots by about one-third.

E

PLANT PROFILE

HEIGHT	90cm (3ft)
SPREAD	60cm (24in)
TYPE	Bush (cluster-flowered)
HARDINESS	Fully hardy
FLOWERING	Summer to autumn

E | 'Ernest H. Morse'

A LOW-GROWING, BRIGHT RED BUSH ROSE, 'Ernest H. Morse'
keeps flowering over summer, with shapely, high-pointed
buds. On opening, the flowers are nicely scented and 13cm
(5in) wide, withstanding rain well, while the leaves are glossy,
dark green and disease-resistant, though they are sometimes
susceptible to mildew. Prune in late winter, removing all
unproductive stems. Cut back the remainder to outward-
facing buds at about 20–25cm (8–10in). This helps prevent the
centre of the bush becoming congested with crisscrossing
shoots. For large, showy flowers prune to two or three buds.

PLANT PROFILE

HEIGHT 75cm (30in)

SPREAD 60cm (24in)

TYPE Bush (large-flowered)

HARDINESS Fully hardy

FLOWERING Summer to autumn

EVELYN ('Aussaucer')

E

INTRODUCED IN 1991, EVELYN mixes the best of old-rose charm and scent (and the scent is wonderfully fruity) with an ability to repeat flower. The large flowers begin with just a faint hint of pink, which gains in intensity in the second half of summer, and the shape, too, can change from a wide, shallow cup to a rosette. Prune the stems in late winter by one-half to two-thirds. Harder pruning gives fewer stems but larger flowers, while lighter pruning gives more flowering stems with slightly smaller blooms.

PLANT PROFILE

HEIGHT 90cm (3ft)

SPREAD 1.1m (3½ft)

TYPE Shrub

HARDINESS Fully hardy

FLOWERING Summer

E | EYE PAINT ('Maceye')

EYE PAINT IS AN APPROPRIATELY VIVID NAME for this rose because the clusters (in varying sizes) of bright red, open flowers have a smart white eye, with yellow stamens right in the middle. Healthy, disease-free, and free-flowering, there is a profusion of blooms and glossy foliage making EYE PAINT an excellent choice for a front-of-border position, or even a colourful, low dividing hedge across the middle of the garden. Cut back the main stems in late winter to 25–45cm (10–18in), and reduce the sideshoots by about one-third of their length.

PLANT PROFILE

HEIGHT 1.1m (3½ft)

SPREAD 75cm (2½ft)

TYPE Bush (cluster-flowered)

HARDINESS Fully hardy

FLOWERING Summer to autumn

'Fantin-Latour'

F

A FAVOURITE AMONG THE ROSE EXPERTS, 'Fantin-Latour' was introduced in 1900. It makes a solid shrub well covered in sweet-scented, petal-packed, large pink flowers and has its one burst of bloom in midsummer. The dark green, leafy growth gives it extra presence and shape. A Centifolia rose, it is named after the 19th-century French artist, Henri Fantin-Latour. Prune to maintain its impressive shrub shape, removing only diseased, dead, and damaged growth, and leaving the old wood intact. Give a minimal late-winter prune to promote a balanced shape.

PLANT PROFILE	
HEIGHT	1.5m (5ft)
SPREAD	1.2m (4ft)
TYPE	Old garden rose
HARDINESS	Fully hardy
FLOWERING	Midsummer

F

'Félicité Parmentier'

WHAT MARKS OUT THIS TOUGH, SCENTED rose is the way its buds fatten and fatten, with a slight yellow tinge, and then open revealing a tight-packed arrangement of light pink petals with a touch of cream at the edges. The shape is upright and compact, and the green leaves have a greyish tinge. An Alba rose, it needs very little attention. To create a large, impressive shrub, remove only diseased, dead, and damaged growth. Give a light trim in late winter to help produce a balanced shape and plenty of flowering stems with smaller blooms. Harder pruning gives fewer stems with larger flowers.

PLANT PROFILE

HEIGHT 1.3m (4½ft)

SPREAD 1.2m (4ft))

TYPE Old garden rose

HARDINESS Fully hardy

FLOWERING Midsummer

'Félicité Perpétue'

F

AN EXCELLENT OLD RAMBLING ROSE, dating back to 1827, this is still a best buy. The prolific small flowers, 4cm (1½in) wide, make a great show of white against the dark green foliage. The growth is vigorous and bushy, forming an impenetrable shape, just right for growing into stout trees, a hedge, over an old wall, or for covering an eyesore. It also grows on cold, shady walls. 'Félicité Perpétue' can even be allowed to mound up on the ground. For the first two years prune sideshoots in late summer by 8cm (3in) to a strong, new shoot. From then on prune up to one-third of the oldest main stems to the ground.

PLANT PROFILE	
HEIGHT	To 5m (15ft)
TYPE	Rambler
HARDINESS	Fully hardy
FLOWERING	Midsummer

F

FELLOWSHIP ('Harwelcome')

AN EXTREMELY RELIABLE ROSE, FELLOWSHIP keeps flowering with incredible freedom right through summer, and rarely presents any problems. The deep orange flowers are not too flashy, and they add a distinctive, colourful note to a mixed rose or border scheme. Even the leaves are healthy and glossy. It is an excellent present for someone completely lacking green fingers. Prune in late winter, cutting back the main stems to 25–45cm (10–18in) above the ground and shortening the sideshoots by approximately one-third.

PLANT PROFILE

HEIGHT 75cm (30in)

SPREAD 60cm (24in)

TYPE Bush (cluster-flowered)

HARDINESS Fully hardy

FLOWERING Summer to autumn

'Ferdinand Pichard'

RED- AND PINK-STRIPED PETALS might sound horribly up-front but, with a pale pink background, this Hybrid Perpetual rose actually looks like a subtle raspberry-ripple ice cream. The effect is balanced by the glossy leaves, while the shape is upright and compact. There is one main flush of richly scented flowers in early summer, with many more following after. In formal gardens prune shoots by one-half to two-thirds in late winter. In less formal and cottage gardens remove only diseased, dead, and damaged growth, and give a light overall prune for shape.

PLANT PROFILE	
HEIGHT	1.5m (5ft)
SPREAD	1.2m (4ft)
TYPE	Old garden rose
HARDINESS	Fully hardy
FLOWERING	Summer to autumn

F

FERDY ('Keitoli')

FINE-CUT LEAVES COVER THE ARCHING STEMS, and make a mound of uneven growth, which is quite spectacular when it erupts in flowers in summer. The blooms are small and tightly packed together and give a frothy, bright pink effect. FERDY is particularly effective beside an artificial pond where you want a colourful, near naturalistic look, and is also good at smothering weeds. Little pruning is needed, but if growth is getting too rampant, cut back each overlong stem to an outward-facing bud in late winter. Shorten sideshoots at the same time if necessary.

PLANT PROFILE

HEIGHT 80cm (32in)

SPREAD 1.2m (4ft)

TYPE Ground-cover

HARDINESS Fully hardy

FLOWERING Summer to autumn

FESTIVAL ('Kordialo')

WINNER OF SOME PRESTIGIOUS ROSE PRIZES, including UK Rose of the Year in 1994, FESTIVAL is highly regarded for the silver colour on the underside of its petals, which are crimson-scarlet above, and also for its abundant, luxuriant, dark green leaves. Give it a prominent position, possibly in a pot, near a focal point such as the base of a statue where it adds a flashy touch. In late winter remove all growth apart from the strongest shoots, and then cut them back by one-third to one-half. This forces up plenty of new, vigorous growth.

PLANT PROFILE	
HEIGHT	60cm (24in)
SPREAD	50cm (20in)
TYPE	Bush (cluster-flowered, patio)
HARDINESS	Fully hardy
FLOWERING	Summer to autumn

F | *filipes* 'Kiftsgate'

A FANTASTICALLY RAMPANT GROWER, *R. filipes* 'Kiftsgate' can be thought of as impressively power-packed or manically over the top. Try it only if you have masses of space because it cannot be restrained. It is normally grown high into a tree from where it often launches into adjacent trees. It can also be roughly trained around a garden boundary where its vicious thorns make an impenetrable barrier. The stunning summer display involves thousands of small creamy-white flowers. Pruning is not necessary, but you can cut one-third of the oldest main stems to ground level annually.

PLANT PROFILE

HEIGHT To 10m (30ft)

TYPE Rambler

HARDINESS Fully hardy

FLOWERING Midsummer; hips in autumn

FRAGRANT CLOUD ('Tanellis')

F

THE SCENT IS SUPERB, the flower shape stylish, the colour stays coral-red and hardly fades, and the foliage is glossy, dark green. In short, FRAGRANT CLOUD is a real winner, with the first buds opening in early summer. Grow it for the show bench and garden, where it can also be trained as a standard. The only minor drawbacks are possible attacks of mildew and black spot. In late winter remove all unproductive stems, and prune hard to outward-facing buds at 20–25cm (8–10in). This helps deter shoots crowding the centre. For large, showy flowers prune harder, to just two or three buds.

PLANT PROFILE

HEIGHT 75cm (30in)

SPREAD 60cm (24in)

TYPE Bush (large-flowered)

HARDINESS Fully hardy

FLOWERING Summer to autumn

F | 'Francis E. Lester'

THE RATHER LAX, VIGOROUS, THORNY STEMS are usually grown into stout, strong trees, or they can be trained through a mixed hedge. 'Francis E. Lester' is also good for covering an eyesore because it is hard to beat for sheer flower power and scent. The pink buds open to white flowers with yellow stamens. The abundant, dark green foliage is another plus. For the first two years prune sideshoots by 8cm (3in) to a vigorous shoot in late summer. From the third year prune up to one-third of the oldest main stems to ground level.

PLANT PROFILE

HEIGHT 5m (15ft)

TYPE Rambler

HARDINESS Fully hardy

FLOWERING Midsummer; hips in autumn

'François Juranville'

F

A TALL RAMBLER, 'François Juranville is perfect for sending up into large, stout trees and covering old ugly sheds. It is extremely vigorous with few thorns and decent-sized flowers. The blooms have a slightly deeper pink tinge in the centre, and give off the scent of fresh apples. Do not be tempted to try it against a small wall because, as one of the most rampant ramblers, it is almost impossible to restrain. In late summer, for the first two years, prune sideshoots by 8cm (3in) to a strong, new shoot. From the third year onwards, prune at most one-third of the oldest main stems back to ground level.

PLANT PROFILE	
HEIGHT 6m (20ft)	
TYPE Rambler	
HARDINESS Fully hardy	
FLOWERING Midsummer	

F 'Frau Karl Druschki'

ONE OF THE BEST AND MOST BEAUTIFUL WHITES, 'Frau Karl Druschki' is a Hybrid Perpetual rose dating back to 1901 and has everything going for it except scent. The buds suggest red flowers because they have a red tinge but they actually open to milky-white. Growth is strong and arching but look out for mildew. It is also known as 'Snow Queen' and 'White American Beauty'. In formal gardens prune shoots by one-half to two-thirds in late winter. In less formal and cottage gardens remove only diseased, dead, and damaged growth, and give a light overall prune for shape.

PLANT PROFILE	
HEIGHT	To 1.5m (5ft)
SPREAD	1.2m (4ft)
TYPE	Old garden rose
HARDINESS	Fully hardy
FLOWERING	Summer to autumn

FREEDOM ('Dicjem')

IF YOU NEED A PROLIFIC SHOW of bright yellow, scented roses all summer at the front of the border or in a mixed rose scheme, this is the rose to go for. It is disease-resistant, vigorous, and bushy, and its rich colour does not fade. Thoroughly reliable, this is a good choice for a new gardener. In late winter, remove all unproductive stems, and prune hard to outward-facing buds, leaving 20–25cm (8–10in) of stem. This helps to keep the centre of the bush clear of crossing shoots. For large, showy flowers prune harder, leaving just two or three buds on each stem.

PLANT PROFILE

HEIGHT	75cm (30in)
SPREAD	60cm (24in)
TYPE	Bush (large-flowered)
HARDINESS	Fully hardy
FLOWERING	Summer to autumn

F 'Fritz Nobis'

A SHAPELY SHRUB WITH A BIG REPUTATION, 'Fritz Nobis' provides an excellent show of clear pink flowers that hang on for a long time in early summer when it is at its peak. Few shrub roses equal its display. These factors, with the large, dark green leaves, vigorous growth, autumn-to-winter show of hips, and gentle scent, make 'Fritz Nobis' a high-class shrub. Remove only diseased, dead, and damaged growth when pruning. Give a late-winter trim to help produce a balanced shape. Harder pruning gives fewer stems with larger flowers, lighter pruning more flowering stems with smaller blooms.

PLANT PROFILE

HEIGHT 2m (6ft)

SPREAD 2m (6ft)

TYPE Shrub

HARDINESS Fully hardy

FLOWERING Summer; hips in autumn to winter

'Fru Dagmar Hastrup'

ONE OF THE BEST OF THE RUGOSA ROSES, 'Fru Dagmar Hastrup' has compact, shrubby growth, dark green leaves, rich pink buds, light pink flowers, and crimson hips. The effectiveness of the red hips is highlighted because they coincide with the final burst of flowers. 'Fru Dagmar Hastrup' is very effective in borders but it also makes an excellent, low-growing, colourful hedge, which is how many prefer to grow it. In late winter prune by one-half to two-thirds. Pruning harder gives fewer stems with larger flowers, while pruning more lightly gives more flowering stems with smaller blooms.

PLANT PROFILE	
HEIGHT 90cm (3ft)	
SPREAD 1.2m (4ft)	
TYPE Shrub	
HARDINESS Fully hardy	
FLOWERING Summer; hips in autumn	

F | 'Frühlingsgold'

A TOP CHOICE FOR A PALE YELLOW ROSE, 'Frühlingsgold' has a wonderful, heavy scent, and can flower from late spring or early summer. It is tough and reliable, with arching branches covered right the way along with flowers that gradually fade to white. Although it flowers for only a few weeks early in the season, it does provide one of the best rose sights of the year. Remove only diseased, dead, and damaged growth when pruning to preserve its shrubby appearance. A minimal late-winter prune also helps to maintain a balanced shape.

PLANT PROFILE

HEIGHT 2.5m (8ft)

SPREAD 2.2m (7ft)

TYPE Shrub

HARDINESS Fully hardy

FLOWERING Late spring to early summer

'Frühlingsmorgen'

F

THE SPRAYS OF LARGE, SCENTED FLOWERS are light pink with primrose-yellow stamens in the centre, and a dash of maroon. While the main flush is in early summer, you will get extra flowers towards the end of summer followed by a few large red hips on the bushy growth. In late winter cut out diseased, dead, and damaged growth. Give a light prune at the same time for a balanced shape. If you prune harder the rose will produce fewer stems with larger flowers.

PLANT PROFILE	
HEIGHT	2m (6ft)
SPREAD	1.5m (5ft)
TYPE	Shrub
HARDINESS	Fully hardy
FLOWERING	Early and late summer; hips in autumn

G *gallica* var. *officinalis* Apothecary's rose, Red rose of Lancaster

THIS ANCIENT GALLICA ROSE dating back to the Middle Ages, and one of the oldest still grown in Europe, is a beautiful midsummer highlight. The prickle-free stems carry pinkish-red flowers, either individually or in clusters of two to four, set against dark green leaves, and followed by orange-red hips. It sometimes suffers from mildew. In late winter remove only diseased, dead, and damaged growth, leaving the old wood intact. If necessary, give a light prune to encourage a balanced shape. A harder prune gives fewer stems with larger flowers.

PLANT PROFILE

HEIGHT 80cm (32in)

SPREAD 90cm (3ft)

TYPE Old garden rose

HARDINESS Fully hardy

FLOWERING Midsummer; hips in autumn

gallica 'Versicolor' Rosa mundi

G

THIS RED- AND PINK-STRIPED ROSE from the 17th century is said to get its name from Henry II's mistress, Fair Rosamund. Small and showy, it can be grown alone or in a row as a mini-hedge, injecting colour into formal and informal schemes. It belongs to the Gallica group of roses, which flower only once in the summer and give a high-impact display. It is richly scented. Prune lightly in late winter, removing only diseased, dead, and damaged wood and, if necessary, trimming the rest back for a balanced shape. If you want fewer stems with larger flowers, prune the stems harder.

PLANT PROFILE	
HEIGHT	80cm (32in)
SPREAD	90cm (3ft)
TYPE	Old garden rose
HARDINESS	Fully hardy
FLOWERING	Midsummer

G | GENTLE TOUCH ('Diclulu')

IDEAL FOR GROWING IN SMALL GARDENS, in pots, or as edging, this delicate rose has gentle sprays of pale salmon-coloured flowers. Each bloom is about 5cm (2in) wide and beautifully shaped, with a high-pointed bud. The dark green leaves help highlight the flowers, which appear right through the summer season. It was UK Rose of the Year in 1986. In late winter prune away all growth apart from the strongest shoots. Cut these back by one-third to one-half to force up plenty of new growth and maintain vigour.

PLANT PROFILE

HEIGHT 50cm (20in)

SPREAD 40cm (16in)

TYPE Bush (cluster-flowered, patio)

HARDINESS Fully hardy

FLOWERING Summer to autumn

GERTRUDE JEKYLL ('Ausbord')

G

GERTRUDE JEKYLL SCORES HIGHER POINTS for its individual flowers than its overall shape. The rich, pink blooms are large and heavy (opening from small buds), and have a strong scent but they do tend to hang down in the rain. While the growth is not exactly neat, it is strong, disease-resistant, and repeat-flowering, making a top-class rose. It is perfect for the back of the border. While the rose is dormant, prune shoots by one-half to two-thirds. Pruning on the lighter side gives more flowering stems with smaller blooms, while harder pruning gives fewer stems with larger flowers.

PLANT PROFILE

HEIGHT	1.5m (5ft)
SPREAD	90cm (3ft)
TYPE	Shrub
HARDINESS	Fully hardy
FLOWERING	Summer to autumn

G | GLAD TIDINGS ('Tantide')

THE GROWTH IS BUSHY AND UPRIGHT, and the long-lasting flowers are beautifully shaped with a striking, bright crimson colour. There are plenty of buds giving excellent coverage. Groups of, say, three or five of these bushes make a striking sight. If you do not mind virtually scentless roses, GLAD TIDINGS has a lot of plusses. Black spot may be a nuisance but it can be tackled by spraying. In late winter cut back the main stems to 25–45cm (10–18in) above the ground, and reduce sideshoots by one-third.

PLANT PROFILE

HEIGHT 80cm (32in)

SPREAD 65cm (26in)

TYPE Bush (cluster-flowered)

HARDINESS Fully hardy

FLOWERING Summer to autumn

glauca

G

EXTREMELY POPULAR, THIS ROSE HAS HEIGHT, grace, and lightness, shooting up out of the ground and then arching over. It has virtually thornless stems and an often open, see-through effect. The leaves are as good as the flowers, being grey-green in light shade (more coppery in direct sun), while the small, gentle pink flowers are single with a white centre. The hips are brownish-red. *R. glauca* adds to the flow of border schemes, unlike those high-profile roses that hog the limelight so that you barely look beyond them. Pruning is unnecessary except for minor trimming for shape.

PLANT PROFILE

HEIGHT 2m (6ft)

SPREAD 1.5m (5ft)

TYPE Wild

HARDINESS Fully hardy

FLOWERING Midsummer; hips in autumn

G | 'Glenfiddich'

ONE OF THE TOP YELLOWS among the cluster-flowered bush roses, 'Glenfiddich' keeps flowering over a long period. The growth is bushy with dark green leaves, and the flowers (which are also good for cutting) appear on straight stems, either individually or grouped in sprays; their amber-enriched colour almost matches the whisky after which 'Glenfiddich' is named. It is a reliable and disease-free rose. Prune in late winter, cutting back the main stems to 25–45cm (10–18in), and shorten sideshoots by about one-third.

PLANT PROFILE

HEIGHT 80cm (32in)	
SPREAD 60cm (24in)	
TYPE Bush (cluster-flowered)	
HARDINESS Fully hardy	
FLOWERING Summer to autumn	

'Gloire de Dijon' Old glory rose

G

ESSENTIAL IN A COTTAGE GARDEN because it has some of the genes of an old garden rose, 'Gloire de Dijon' sends up vigorous stems covered in fat buds in early summer. The large buff-yellow flowers (with a touch of pink) have a strong, rich scent. After the first main burst of flowers, more follow, giving a constant show. Bend down the first stems to force up new growth and prevent the rose from being bare low down. Do not prune for the first two years, but from then on prune in the autumn, after flowering, nipping back the main stems if they are too long and shortening sideshoots by two-thirds.

PLANT PROFILE	
HEIGHT	5m (15ft)
TYPE	Climber
HARDINESS	Fully hardy
FLOWERING	Summer to autumn

G | GOLDEN CELEBRATION ('Ausgold')

ONE OF THE BEST YELLOWS AT THIS HEIGHT, this rose has nothing but good qualities – a gentle arching shape, vigorous growth, disease-resistance, and very large, strongly scented flowers with a rich colour. GOLDEN CELEBRATION makes an attractive centrepiece in any bed. To enhance its impressive shrub shape, remove only diseased, dead, and damaged growth, and leave the old wood intact. Give a minimal prune in late winter for a balanced outline. If you prune harder, fewer stems with larger flowers will result; lighter pruning produces more flowering stems with smaller blooms.

PLANT PROFILE

HEIGHT 1.2m (4ft)

SPREAD 1.2m (4ft)

TYPE Shrub

HARDINESS Fully hardy

FLOWERING Summer

'Golden Showers'

THE SCENTED, YELLOW FLOWERS of 'Golden Showers' give a remarkably continuous show all summer, backed up by the glossy foliage. Growth is not that high, making it ideal for average-size walls and posts. Train it around and up posts, or out horizontally along walls to force up new growth; if 'Golden Showers' is allowed to grow straight up, the lower growth will be bare with all the flowers high at the top. Allow the plant to establish by not pruning for the first two years and then start to prune in the autumn, after flowering, cutting back the main stems and shortening sideshoots by two-thirds.

PLANT PROFILE	
HEIGHT	3m (10ft)
TYPE	Climber
HARDINESS	Fully hardy
FLOWERING	Summer to autumn

G | GOLDEN WEDDING ('Arokris')

FLOWERING RIGHT THROUGH THE SUMMER, this rose is equally reliable outside and indoors as a cut flower. The blooms are on the large side, being stylish, bright, and showy, while the foliage is attractively glossy. The bushy, vigorous growth compensates for the lack of any discernible scent. These excellent qualities mean that the popularity of GOLDEN WEDDING is not due just to its name, though it does make a very good anniversary gift. In late winter cut back the main stems to 25–45cm (10–18in), and reduce the sideshoots by about one-third of their length.

PLANT PROFILE

HEIGHT 90cm (3ft)

SPREAD 75cm (30in)

TYPE Bush (cluster-flowered)

HARDINESS Fully hardy

FLOWERING Summer

'Golden Wings'

WITH AN OPEN, SAUCER-LIKE SHAPE, the flowers of GOLDEN WINGS have an amber centre surrounded by 5–10 pale yellow petals. They withstand inclement weather and keep appearing right through summer if the old ones are promptly removed as they fade. The scent is often described as delicious and refreshing. This rose is disease-resistant and totally reliable. Pruning is minimal. Remove only diseased, dead, and damaged growth, and leave the old wood intact. Cut back overlong shoots in late winter for a balanced shape. If you prune harder, the result will be fewer stems with larger flowers.

G

PLANT PROFILE

HEIGHT	1.5m (5ft)
SPREAD	1.3m (4½ft)
TYPE	Shrub
HARDINESS	Fully hardy
FLOWERING	Summer to autumn

G | 'Goldfinch'

A GOOD CHOICE OF RAMBLER if you don't want one that shoots out in all directions making tangled growth in trees. 'Goldfinch' is much more restrained, being valued for its thornless stems, glossy leaves, deep yellow flowers fading to white, and fruity scent. It makes a lovely addition to a mixed hedge though it can also be grown as a large shrub. For the first two years only, in late summer, prune sideshoots by 8cm (3in) to a strong, new shoot. From then on prune at most one-third of the oldest main stems back to ground level.

PLANT PROFILE

HEIGHT 2.5m (8ft)

TYPE Rambler

HARDINESS Fully hardy

FLOWERING Midsummer

GRAHAM THOMAS ('Ausmas')

G

A HIGHLY VALUED ROSE named after a great rose expert, GRAHAM THOMAS has a long list of attractions. It combines pure yellow flowers with the look of an old garden rose, a deep scent, vigorous, upright growth, and a flowering season lasting from early summer into the start of autumn. It makes an excellent centrepiece in a bed in formal and cottage gardens. In late winter prune stems by one-half to two-thirds. The harder you prune, the fewer the stems and the larger the flowers; lighter pruning results in the reverse.

PLANT PROFILE	
HEIGHT 1.2m (4ft)	
SPREAD 1.5m (5ft)	
TYPE Shrub	
HARDINESS Fully hardy	
FLOWERING Summer to autumn	

G | 'Grandpa Dickson'

QUITE A SHORT, UPRIGHT PLANT, this takes up very little space with its large, shapely, pale yellow flowers. It can easily be incorporated in any scheme with annuals, and keeps the planting alive with its long flowering season. 'Grandpa Dickson' withstands bad weather but lacks only one thing: a decent scent. To encourage plenty of new shoots and an open-centred bush shape, prune in late winter by removing all unproductive stems, and cutting hard to outward-facing buds at 20–25cm (8–10in). For large, showy flowers prune harder, leaving just two or three buds.

PLANT PROFILE

HEIGHT	75cm (30in)
SPREAD	60cm (24in)
TYPE	Bush (large-flowered)
HARDINESS	Fully hardy
FLOWERING	Summer to autumn

'Great Maiden's Blush'

A LARGE, BRANCHING, ARCHING SHRUB for the back of
the border or an informal perimeter hedge, 'Great Maiden's
Blush' has grey-green leaves and a gentle pink colour on
opening, fading to pinkish-white. It gives a substantial show
in the middle of the summer, when the scent leans more to
the sweet and refined than the strong. It is listed under Alba
roses in most catalogues. Remove only diseased, dead, and
damaged growth when pruning, and cut back lightly in late
winter to produce a balanced shape. Harder pruning gives
fewer stems with larger flowers.

PLANT PROFILE	
HEIGHT 2m (6ft)	
SPREAD 1.3m (4½ft)	
TYPE Old garden rose	
HARDINESS Fully hardy	
FLOWERING Midsummer	

G | GROUSE ('Korimro')

ALMOST THE ULTIMATE GROUND-COVER ROSE, GROUSE does
not get above knee-high and spreads out widely and rapidly in
all directions. Unlike many so-called ground-cover roses,
which have wide, gappy growth, this smothers any weeds
beneath. The small flowers (appearing in mid- and late
summer) are pale pink, verging on white, and the leaves glossy,
dark green. GROUSE can also be grown to spread down banks
and hang over walls. Little pruning is required, but if growth is
too rampant cut back to an outward-facing bud in late winter.
Shorten sideshoots at the same time if necessary.

PLANT PROFILE

HEIGHT 60cm (24in)

SPREAD 3m (10ft)

TYPE Ground-cover

HARDINESS Fully hardy

FLOWERING Summer

'Gruss an Aachen'

G

IT MAY BE ON THE SMALL SIDE, but 'Gruss an Aachen' certainly has high-quality flowers. They look like those of an old garden rose and start off light pink, gradually fading to soft creamy-white. In addition, 'Gruss an Aachen' has a long flowering season and the scent is very good, making it an excellent choice for a front-of-border scheme. Despite having been around since 1909 it is still not that widely grown, but it is well worth trying, especially in small gardens. In late winter cut back main stems to 25–45cm (10–18in) above the ground, and reduce sideshoots by about one-third of their length.

PLANT PROFILE

HEIGHT 75cm (2½ft)

SPREAD 90cm (3ft)

TYPE Bush (cluster-flowered)

HARDINESS Frost hardy

FLOWERING Summer to autumn

G | 'Guinée'

IF YOU WANT LARGE, DARK RED FLOWERS and a terrific scent, this climber scores very high marks. The early summer flush of blooms is the best. Plant it where you can appreciate the scent and, for the best effect, give it a light background and pamper it with rich soil. For the first two years simply train new shoots into a horizontal position to produce flowering sideshoots. From the third year prune in the autumn, after flowering, nipping back the main stems if they are too long, and shortening sideshoots by two-thirds.

PLANT PROFILE
HEIGHT 5m (15ft)
TYPE Climber
HARDINESS Fully hardy
FLOWERING Summer

'Hakuun'

II

A VERY USEFUL EDGING PLANT with bushy growth, 'Hakuun' can also be grown in pots. There have been dozens of more recent patio roses (this is a 1962 introduction), but most tend to be brightly coloured reds or soft, quiet pinks, making this white still a good buy. The flowers have an orange-yellow tinge on opening, which quickly fades to creamy-white (the translation of the Japanese name 'Hakuun' is white cloud). Prune in late winter, selecting the strongest shoots and removing the rest. Shorten the selected shoots by one-third to one-half to force up plenty of new, vigorous growth.

PLANT PROFILE	
HEIGHT 40cm (16in)	
SPREAD 45cm (18in)	
TYPE Bush (cluster-flowered, patio)	
HARDINESS Fully hardy	
FLOWERING Summer to autumn	

H | HAMPSHIRE ('Korhamp')

A MODEST GROUND-COVER ROSE, HAMPSHIRE makes a knee-high, spreading mound covered with 5cm (2in) wide, open, scarlet flowers. They have a striking yellow centre that gradually fades to white. HAMPSHIRE also offers a long flowering season, glossy leaves, and an attractive display of orange hips. Little pruning is needed, but if growth is getting much too rampant, cut back stems to an outward-facing bud in late winter. At the same time shorten the sideshoots if they are becoming too long.

PLANT PROFILE

HEIGHT 30cm (12in)

SPREAD 75cm (30in)

TYPE Ground-cover

HARDINESS Fully hardy

FLOWERING Summer to autumn; hips in autumn

HANDEL ('Macha')

H

IDEAL FOR PILLARS AND POSTS and growing up small arches, this superb mini-climber reaches 3m (10ft). The almost-scentless flowers are creamy-white and stand out because they are pink right around the edge. In the hottest part of summer the pink colour tends to intensify and sometimes even spreads. After the first main crop of flowers the display continues. For the first two years train new shoots into a horizontal position. From the third year prune in the autumn, after flowering, nipping back the main stems if necessary and shortening sideshoots by two-thirds.

PLANT PROFILE	
HEIGHT 3m (10ft)	
TYPE Climber	
HARDINESS Fully hardy	
FLOWERING Summer to autumn	

H | HANNAH GORDON ('Korweiso')

SLIGHTLY SMALLER THAN MOST ROSES in this category, HANNAH GORDON makes an attractive, bushy plant with a spreading, open shape well covered in dark green leaves. The buds are plump, the flowers large, the scent delicate, and the sprays keep appearing all summer. It is a very useful rose at the front of a bed or border, though it can also be grown in a large tub or urn in a courtyard scheme. In late winter, cut back the main stems to 25–45cm (10–18in) above the ground, and prune sideshoots by about one-third of their length.

PLANT PROFILE

HEIGHT 80cm (32in)

SPREAD 65cm (26in)

TYPE Bush (cluster-flowered)

HARDINESS Fully hardy

FLOWERING Summer to autumn

'Harry Wheatcroft'

H

GOOD FUN, EVEN OUTRAGEOUS, this brightly coloured rose has a mix of red, yellow, and orange stripes and streaks on its petals while the undersides are yellow. Forget the lack of scent and the tendency to mildew, this is a brash rose with a high-pointed flower shape before it fully opens, and the ability to withstand rain. The leaves are glossy, reddish-green. In late winter remove all unproductive stems, and prune the rest hard to outward-facing buds, leaving 20–25cm (8–10in) of stem. This helps discourage crisscrossing shoots in the centre. For large, showy flowers prune harder, to just two or three buds.

PLANT PROFILE

HEIGHT 90cm (3ft)

SPREAD 60cm (24in)

TYPE Bush (large-flowered)

HARDINESS Fully hardy

FLOWERING Summer to autumn

H | 'Henri Martin' Red moss rose

A GOOD CHOICE FOR A SHADY, COLD WALL, although it performs far better in the sun, 'Henri Martin' has lovely, 8cm (3in) wide, scented flowers of the richest, near-crimson red. The growth is arching, graceful, and nearly thorn-free, with dark green leaves. 'Henri Martin' is listed in many catalogues with the Moss roses because of the attractive, small, moss-like growth on the stems and buds. Remove only diseased, dead, and damaged growth, and give a minimal late-winter prune for shape. Harder pruning gives fewer stems with larger flowers, lighter pruning more stems with smaller blooms.

PLANT PROFILE

HEIGHT To 2m (6ft)

SPREAD 1.2m (4ft)

TYPE Old garden rose

HARDINESS Fully hardy

FLOWERING Summer

HERITAGE ('Ausblush)

GROWING SATISFYINGLY, BUSHILY UPRIGHT, this rose has cupped, light pink, lemon-scented flowers that are almost white at the edge. The flowers keep appearing over the summer, with some still hanging on in the autumn, and the stems are virtually thorn-free. HERITAGE adds a strong presence to pastel-coloured schemes because of its large, 11cm (4½in) wide flowers. In late winter prune shoots by one-half to two-thirds. Pruning hard gives fewer stems with larger flowers, while pruning more lightly results in more flowering stems with smaller blooms.

PLANT PROFILE	
HEIGHT 1.2m (4ft)	
SPREAD 1.2m (4ft)	
TYPE Shrub	
HARDINESS Fully hardy	
FLOWERING Summer to autumn	

H | 'Hermosa'

AN EXQUISITE, MEDIUM-SIZED CHINA ROSE dating back to
1840, 'Hermosa' is known for its small, pale pink, lightly
scented flowers with 35 petals. They keep appearing over a
long period from summer to autumn. The buds are high-
pointed and attractive, appearing on bushy growth with just a
few prickles and grey-green leaves. To make any impact in
large schemes it needs to be planted in groups of, say, three or
five. When pruning, remove only diseased, dead, and damaged
growth, and leave the old wood intact. A minimal late-winter
prune also helps produce a balanced shape.

PLANT PROFILE

HEIGHT 90cm (3ft)

SPREAD 60cm (24in)

TYPE Old garden rose

HARDINESS Fully hardy

FLOWERING Summer to autumn

HERTFORDSHIRE ('Kortenay')

H

HERTFORDSHIRE WILL NICELY FILL A BORDER GAP with its flat, wide-open pink flowers, which are yellow in the centre, set against bright green leaves. Growth is quite dense and will block out weeds after two to three seasons when it has had a chance to really fill out. Initially, though, you will have to weed under and round it, but note that it is quite prickly. It has good disease-resistance. Little pruning is needed, but if growth is too rampant cut it back to outward-facing buds in late winter. Shorten sideshoots at the same time if necessary.

PLANT PROFILE

HEIGHT 45cm (18in)

SPREAD 90cm (3ft)

TYPE Ground-cover

HARDINESS Fully hardy

FLOWERING Summer to autumn

H | HIGH HOPES ('Haryup')

WITH BEAUTIFUL, SHAPELY FLOWERS and a sweet scent over a
long period, HIGH HOPES is a fairly recent (1992), highly
successful introduction. It is perfect for a medium-high
doorway, arch, pillar, or pergola. Growth is quite flexible and
easily trained, modest, and will not romp away in a tangled
mess; it gives decent results even in relatively poor conditions.
Avoid pruning for the first two years, but train new shoots
horizontally to produce flowering sideshoots. From then on,
prune in the autumn, after flowering, cutting back the main
stems as needed and shortening sideshoots by two-thirds.

PLANT PROFILE	
HEIGHT 4m (12ft)	
TYPE Climber	
HARDINESS Fully hardy	
FLOWERING Summer to autumn	

ICEBERG ('Korbin')

AN EXTREMELY POPULAR ROSE, it provides continuous flowers all summer and into autumn. The buds have a pink tinge but the flowers are actually clear white. Anyone who snobbishly thinks a popular rose must be completely lacking in style is totally wrong when it comes to ICEBERG. Plant it among beautiful red and pink roses and you will get an excellent combination. In late winter cut back the main stems to 25–45cm (10–18in) above ground, and shorten sideshoots by about one-third. ICEBERG can also be grown as a standard and there is a climbing version, reaching about 3m (10ft) high.

I

PLANT PROFILE

HEIGHT 80cm (32in)

SPREAD 65cm (26in)

TYPE Bush (cluster-flowered)

HARDINESS Fully hardy

FLOWERING Summer to autumn

INGRID BERGMAN ('Poulman')

THE RED FLOWERS ARE DARK, the petals velvety, the scent refreshing, and the leaves dark green and leathery. In addition, new buds keep appearing all summer long on the strong, branching growth. INGRID BERGMAN, introduced in 1984, is a good performer and provides superb, sumptuous blooms for cut-flower displays. Prune in late winter, removing unproductive stems altogether, and cut back the remainder to outward-pointing buds at 20–25cm (8–10in). This helps to eliminate crossing shoots in the centre of the bush. For large, showy flowers prune harder to two or three buds.

PLANT PROFILE

HEIGHT 80cm (32in)

SPREAD 65cm (26in)

TYPE Bush (large-flowered)

HARDINESS Fully hardy

FLOWERING Summer to autumn

INTRIGUE ('Korlech')

SMALL, BUSHY, AND UPRIGHT, INTRIGUE has dark red, citrus-scented flowers. If you like the initial high-pointed flower shape of large-flowered bush roses, and want them in big numbers, try this rose. The blooms appear in clusters all summer and beyond, and are great for cutting. The leaves are glossy, purplish-red. INTRIGUE guarantees good colour at the front of a border. Cut back the main stems to 25–45cm (10–18in) above the ground in late winter, and shorten sideshoots by about one-third.

PLANT PROFILE	
HEIGHT	70cm (28in)
SPREAD	60cm (24in)
TYPE	Bush (cluster-flowered)
HARDINESS	Frost hardy
FLOWERING	Summer to autumn

I

INVINCIBLE ('Runatru')

A SMALL BUSH ROSE with glossy, dark green foliage and
clusters of bright crimson flowers all summer long, this looks
as good in the garden as it does when brightening up cut-
flower displays. If you need a medium-high red, it will not let
you down. The overall shape is bushy and compact, and the
leaves are disease-resistant. In late winter cut back the main
stems to 25–45cm (10–18in), and reduce the sideshoots by
about one-third of their length.

PLANT PROFILE

HEIGHT 70cm (28in)

SPREAD 50cm (20in)

TYPE Bush (cluster-flowered)

HARDINESS Fully hardy

FLOWERING Summer to autumn

'Ispahan'

I

'ISPAHAN' HAS ONE OF THE LONGEST DISPLAYS of any old garden rose, and mixes clusters of clear pink flowers with a lovely scent. At 1.5m (5ft) high, this Damask rose is usually grown towards the back of the border and is superb in cottage and formal gardens. Growth is bushy and upright, and the stems are virtually thornless. When pruning remove only diseased, dead, and damaged growth. A gentle trim in late winter also helps produce a balanced shape. Light pruning will produce more flowering stems with smaller blooms, while harder pruning gives fewer stems with larger flowers.

PLANT PROFILE	
HEIGHT 1.5m (5ft)	
SPREAD 1.2m (4ft)	
TYPE Old garden rose	
HARDINESS Fully hardy	
FLOWERING Summer	

J

JACQUELINE DU PRÉ ('Harwanna')

WITH ITS WIDE-OPEN FLOWERS set against dark green, glossy leaves, this rose provides colour right through the growing season. The golden-centred flowers never let up, growth is bushy and vigorous, and if only the gentle scent were stronger JACQUELINE DU PRÉ would have everything. Still, it is a high-performance shrub for any scheme. Prune out diseased, dead, and damaged growth, and leave the old wood intact. Give a minimal late-winter prune to help produce a balanced shape; the harder you prune, the fewer the stems, but the larger the blooms.

PLANT PROFILE

HEIGHT 1.2m (4ft)

SPREAD 90cm (3ft)

TYPE Shrub

HARDINESS Fully hardy

FLOWERING Early summer to autumn

'Julia's Rose'

J

THE COLOUR IS EXTREMELY UNUSUAL, being a mix of copper and faded brown, and is hard to pin down. 'Julia's Rose' is well worth trying but do note that it needs pampering and a protected site, and the growth is spindly with sparse, reddish-green leaves. In late winter, remove all the unproductive stems, and prune the rest hard to outward-facing buds at 20–25cm (8–10in). This discourages shoots from crowding the centre. For large, showy flowers prune harder, to two or three buds.

PLANT PROFILE	
HEIGHT	75cm (30in)
SPREAD	45cm (18in)
TYPE	Bush (large-flowered)
HARDINESS	Fully hardy
FLOWERING	Summer to autumn

J

'Just Joey'

VOTED THE WORLD'S FAVOURITE ROSE in 1994, 'Just Joey' is a bright and breezy rose, still justifiably popular, and has a highly distinctive colour, being copper-pink, even orange, with frilly edges. There is nothing precious about it, and it will flower reliably right through and beyond summer, the blooms withstanding soaking downpours. When pruning you are aiming for an open-centred bush shape. Remove unproductive stems in late winter and cut the remaining stems to outward-facing buds at 20–25cm (8–10in) from the ground. For large, showy flowers prune harder, leaving just two or three buds.

PLANT PROFILE	
HEIGHT 75cm (30in)	
SPREAD 70cm (28in)	
TYPE Bush (large-flowered)	
HARDINESS Fully hardy	
FLOWERING Summer to autumn	

'Kathleen Harrop'

K

ITS CLUSTERS OF SCENTED, PALE PINK FLOWERS and thornless stems make this rose a very decent alternative to the slightly more vigorous, deep pink climber 'Zéphirine Drouhin' (*see page 314*), especially for a cold, shady site. Mildew can strike when it is against a wall; good air circulation is the solution. Train new shoots horizontally for the first two years. In the following years, prune after flowering, nipping back the main stems and shortening sideshoots by two-thirds. With pruning it can be kept as a 2.5m (8ft) shrub: cut back shoots by one-half to two-thirds after flowering.

PLANT PROFILE

HEIGHT 3m (10ft)

TYPE Climber

HARDINESS Fully hardy

FLOWERING Summer to autumn

K

KATHRYN MORLEY ('Ausclub')

AN UPRIGHT ROSE combining repeat-flowering with the charm and scent of an old garden rose, KATHRYN MORLEY has flowers of soft pink petals held in a cupped shape. Just right for cottage gardens, it has gentle informality, vigorous growth, and an upright shape. It is the ideal ingredient in an easy-going, unobtrusive scheme where there is plenty of colour all summer. In late winter prune shoots by one-half to two-thirds. Harder pruning gives fewer stems with larger flowers, lighter pruning more flowering stems with smaller blooms.

PLANT PROFILE

HEIGHT 90cm (3ft)

SPREAD 90cm (3ft)

TYPE Shrub

HARDINESS Fully hardy

FLOWERING Summer

KEEPSAKE ('Kormalda')

K

THE RICH PINK FLOWERS OF KEEPSAKE will stand out in any scheme, and withstand heavy rain. They are large, at 12cm (5in) wide, with the faintest scent, and make good cut flowers because they last well in water and have an attractive, even shape. If grown where there is shade in late afternoon, the pink of the flowers will appear even stronger. Its uneven, untidy growth gives it an informal, cottage-garden feel. In late winter, remove all unproductive stems, and prune the remainder hard to outward-facing buds at 20–25cm (8–10in). For large, showy flowers prune harder, to two or three buds.

PLANT PROFILE	
HEIGHT	75cm (30in)
SPREAD	60cm (24in)
TYPE	Bush (large-flowered)
HARDINESS	Fully hardy
FLOWERING	Summer to autumn

K | KENT ('Poulcov')

PROLIFICALLY COVERED IN SMALL WHITE FLOWERS with a yellow eye, and tight-packed foliage, 'Kent' makes dense, bushy growth that will keep down weeds well or fill a small gap at the front of a border. Unlike some ground-cover roses, it does not make an open, unpredictable sprawl but quite a neat, compact shape. It is never out of flower over summer. Minimal pruning is needed; if growth is getting too rampant cut back the main shoots to outward-facing buds in late winter. Sideshoots can also be shortened then if necessary.

PLANT PROFILE

HEIGHT	45cm (18in)
SPREAD	90cm (3ft)
TYPE	Ground-cover
HARDINESS	Fully hardy
FLOWERING	Summer to autumn

'Königen von Dänemark'

K

ALSO KNOWN AS QUEEN OF DENMARK, this soft pink Alba rose makes a marvellous show in an old garden rose scheme. The flowers open well clear of the foliage, their initial colour is vivid red before turning pink, the scent is sweet, the leaves are blue-green, and the growth is upright and open. 'Königin von Dänemark' is very highly regarded by rose experts, and makes a fine midsummer show at the back of a border. When pruning in late winter remove diseased, dead, and damaged growth, and trim to a balanced shape. If you prune harder, fewer stems with larger flowers will result.

PLANT PROFILE	
HEIGHT 1.5m (5ft)	
SPREAD 1.2m (4ft)	
TYPE Old garden rose	
HARDINESS Fully hardy	
FLOWERING Midsummer	

K

'Korresia'

GENERALLY RECKONED TO BE THE BEST YELLOW you can buy in this group of bush roses, 'Korresia' bears bright-coloured flowers in sprays regularly over the summer. Each bloom is 8cm (3in) wide with wavy-edged petals and is lightly scented. With good disease-resistance, 'Korresia' makes a failsafe present for a novice gardener who needs high-performance plants that do not require any pampering. In late winter cut back the main stems to 25–45cm (10–18in) above the ground, and shorten the sideshoots by about one-third.

PLANT PROFILE

HEIGHT 75cm (30in)

SPREAD 60cm (24in)

TYPE Bush (cluster-flowered)

HARDINESS Fully hardy

FLOWERING Summer to autumn

L. D. Braithwaite ('Auscrim')

L

An excellent, bright-red-flowering bushy plant,
L. D. Braithwaite has a scent that is soft and lovely rather
than knock-out (being stronger when it is fully open). Its
uneven, loose growth is very much part of its appeal. It is
a strong performer that mixes well with old garden roses
and is nicely covered in flowers all summer. In late winter
prune shoots by one-half to two-thirds. Harder pruning
gives fewer stems with larger flowers, and lighter pruning
more flowering stems with slightly smaller blooms.

PLANT PROFILE

HEIGHT 1.1m (3½ft)

SPREAD 1.1m (3½ft)

TYPE Shrub

HARDINESS Fully hardy

FLOWERING Summer to autumn

L | L'AIMANT ('Harzola')

FREE-FLOWERING AND DISEASE-RESISTANT, L'AIMANT scores high points all round. Its flowers are a lovely, warm shade of pink with reddish overtones, making it stand out from other softer, quieter pinks. The scented flowers look equally delightful in the garden and in a cut-flower display, where it is particularly valued for its array of about 30 petals. Overall growth is vigorous and hard to fault. Cut back the main stems in late winter to 25–45cm (10–18in) above the ground, and reduce the sideshoots by about one-third of their length.

PLANT PROFILE	
HEIGHT 90cm (3ft)	
SPREAD 75cm (30in)	
TYPE Bush (cluster-flowered)	
HARDINESS Fully hardy	
FLOWERING Summer to autumn	

LAURA FORD ('Chewarvel')

CALLING IT A CLIMBER might sound a bit ambitious for
something that barely zooms past the scalp of an American
basketball player, but a climber it is, and just right for training
up and round poles and the verticals on a pergola. The rich
yellow flowers appear in clusters and have a faint fruity scent,
while the leaves are glossy. If you need a restrained, brightly
coloured climber, it is a great choice. Do not prune for the
first two years, but train new shoots into a horizontal position.
From the third year on, prune after flowering, nipping back
overlong main stems, and shortening sideshoots by two-thirds.

L

PLANT PROFILE

HEIGHT 2.2m (7ft)

TYPE Climber

HARDINESS Fully hardy

FLOWERING Summer to autumn

L | LEAPING SALMON ('Peamight')

WITH THE HIGH-POINTED FLOWER SHAPE of a large-flowered rose, LEAPING SALMON is 3m (10ft) tall, and just right for a pillar or arch. The scent is rich and sweet, the flowers large and long lasting when cut, and the glossy foliage is disease-resistant. The young stems need to be gently and horizontally trained against a wall when still young and flexible, before they quickly stiffen, to encourage more flowering shoots. From the third year onwards prune in the autumn, after flowering, nipping back the main stems if necessary and shortening sideshoots by two-thirds.

PLANT PROFILE

HEIGHT 3m (10ft)

TYPE Climber

HARDINESS Fully hardy

FLOWERING Summer

'Leverkusen'

L

A DUAL-PURPOSE, VIGOROUS, ARCHING CLIMBER, it can also be pruned and kept on the short side making a very good shrub. Either way, it is known for its healthy, glossy leaves and clusters of lightly citrus-scented, pale yellow flowers, 8cm (3in) wide. There is one main burst of flowers, then a later scattering of blooms. For the first two years train new shoots into a horizontal position. From then on prune in the autumn, after flowering, nipping back the main stems if necessary and shortening sideshoots by two-thirds.

PLANT PROFILE

HEIGHT 3m (10ft)

TYPE Climber

HARDINESS Fully hardy

FLOWERING Summer to autumn

L 'Little White Pet'

A VIGOROUS DISPLAY OF PINK BUDS is followed by the paler flowers, which look a bit like pompoms. Also known as 'White Pet', it is related to 'Félicité Perpétue' (*see page 107*) but is much smaller, making a mounded shrub for the front of the border. 'Little White Pet' is typically grown in cottage or informal gardens, and makes a colourful edging plant beside an artificial pond. Prune in late winter, removing diseased, dead, and damaged growth, and leave the old wood intact. Prune lightly to create a balanced shape; harder pruning gives fewer stems with larger flowers.

PLANT PROFILE

HEIGHT 45cm (18in)

SPREAD 55cm (22in)

TYPE Shrub

HARDINESS Fully hardy

FLOWERING Summer to autumn

'Louise Odier'

A WONDERFUL, OPULENT ROSE, 'Louise Odier' has large, scented, camellia-like flowers, 9cm (3½in) wide. In fact, they are so heavy that they bend down after the rain, but that is just part of their informal charm. 'Louise Odier' belongs to the Bourbon group and has typically tight-packed, scrunched-up petals, in this case with a dash of lilac. Growth is so vigorous that if it is grown against a wall and trained up, with no pruning, it makes a mini-climber. For a freestanding bush prune in late winter, cutting shoots by one-half to two-thirds.

PLANT PROFILE

HEIGHT 2m (6ft)

SPREAD 1.2m (4ft)

TYPE Old garden rose

HARDINESS Fully hardy

FLOWERING Summer to autumn

L | LOVING MEMORY ('Korgund')

THE FLOWERS ARE SYMMETRICALLY SHAPED, and the petals are a beautiful shade of dark red. They are held on strong, upright stems and always make a good show, though the scent is not strong. A medium-high beauty, LOVING MEMORY is also good for cut flowers. Remove all unproductive stems in late winter, and prune the rest to outward-facing buds at 20–25cm (8–10in). This helps produce a vigorous, open-centred bush. Pruning harder, to just two or three buds, produces large, showy flowers.

PLANT PROFILE

HEIGHT 1.1m (3½ft)

SPREAD 75cm (2½ft)

TYPE Bush (large-flowered)

HARDINESS Fully hardy

FLOWERING Summer to autumn

'Madame Alfred Carrière'

M

ONE OF THE BIG NAMES in the rose world, 'Madame Alfred Carrière' produces an overwhelming initial show followed by many more flowers. The sweetly scented blooms are cream on opening, gradually turning pinkish-white. This rose can be grown on a cold, shady wall, or be pruned and grown as a massive shrub, 3m (10ft) high. Avoid pruning for the first two years, but train new shoots into a horizontal position to produce flowering sideshoots. From then on, prune in the autumn, nipping back the main stems if necessary and shortening sideshoots by two-thirds.

PLANT PROFILE	
HEIGHT	5m (15ft)
TYPE	Climber
HARDINESS	Fully hardy
FLOWERING	Summer to autumn

M | 'Madame de Sancy de Parabère'

ALTHOUGH IT FLOWERS ONLY ONCE, in early summer, this climber has clear pink blooms that are large at 12cm (5in) wide. Look closely and you will see that the outer petals are larger than the inner ones, making an attractive rosette in the centre. The leaves are dark green, and the arching stems are thorn-free. Some catalogues list 'Madame de Sancy de Parabère' as a rambler. For the first two years train new shoots horizontally to produce flowering sideshoots. From the third year prune in the autumn, trimming back the main stems if they are too long and shortening sideshoots by two-thirds.

PLANT PROFILE

HEIGHT 5m (15ft)

TYPE Climber

HARDINESS Frost hardy

FLOWERING Early summer

'Madame Grégoire Staechelin'

M

A POWERHOUSE OF A CLIMBER, 'Madame Grégoire Staechelin' has one great big burst of flowers in early summer in a first-rate display. The long buds open, revealing pink petals with a reddish tinge beneath, and the scent is superb. Do not snip off the fading flowers, even if you can reach them, because they are followed by attractive hips. This is a good choice for a cold, shady wall. Avoid pruning for the first two years but train new shoots horizontally. Prune in the autumn from the third year by nipping back the main stems and shortening sideshoots by two-thirds.

PLANT PROFILE

HEIGHT 6m (20ft)

TYPE Climber

HARDINESS Fully hardy

FLOWERING Early summer; hips in autumn

M | 'Madame Hardy'

GIVEN A SUNNY, SHELTERED POSITION, this is one of the stars of the white old garden roses. Beautiful and scented, 'Madame Hardy' is a superb Damask rose. When the buds open in midsummer for the once-only show of flowers there is a tinge of pink, but they quickly turn pure white with a tiny green eye. The white stands out best against an adjacent rich red rose. Growth is vigorous, dense, and prickly. Remove diseased, dead, and damaged growth in late winter, and trim for a balanced shape. Harder pruning gives fewer stems with larger flowers, and lighter pruning the reverse.

PLANT PROFILE	
HEIGHT	1.5m (5ft)
SPREAD	1.2m (4ft)
TYPE	Old garden rose
HARDINESS	Fully hardy
FLOWERING	Summer

'Madame Isaac Pereire'

M

NOTHING SUCCEEDS LIKE EXCESS. This Bourbon rose has everything you need from an old garden rose, especially the scent, which takes some beating. Each flower is a full 15cm (6in) wide, with the petals tightly packed together in a cupped shape; the late summer show is every bit as good as the first. The leaves are also large, while growth is so vigorous and arching that 'Madame Isaac Pereire' is on the verge of being a climber. If you can support the stems, even in the informality of a cottage garden, so much the better. In late winter prune shoots by one-half to two-thirds.

PLANT PROFILE

HEIGHT 2.2m (7ft)

SPREAD 2m (6ft)

TYPE Old garden rose

HARDINESS Fully hardy

FLOWERING Summer to autumn

M | 'Madame Knorr'

BELONGING TO THE PORTLAND GROUP, 'Madame Knorr' has the characteristically rich scent and look of an old garden rose. The flowers are large, at 10cm (4in) wide, and the pink petals have a distinctive lilac tinge; each bloom is slightly darker in the centre. There is one main flush of flowers in midsummer followed by further scatterings but, because 'Madame Knorr' is a bushy, leafy plant, it always looks attractive. Prune in late winter, cutting back stems by one-half to two-thirds. Harder pruning gives fewer stems with larger flowers, and lighter pruning more flowering stems with smaller blooms.

PLANT PROFILE

HEIGHT 1.2m (4ft)

SPREAD 90cm (3ft)

TYPE Old garden rose

HARDINESS Fully hardy

FLOWERING Summer to autumn

'Madame Pierre Oger'

M

AN EXCELLENT PLANT FOR A COTTAGE GARDEN, 'Madame Pierre Oger' has clusters of cupped, sweet-scented flowers. Rose experts are quick to point out the beauty of its colouring, which turns darker by a couple of notches in hot sun, while others are more concerned with possible attacks of black spot. But for a profusion of flowers over a long period, this Bourbon rose is a very good choice. In late winter prune by one-half to two-thirds, cutting back harder to produce fewer stems with larger flowers, and more lightly to gain more flowering stems with smaller blooms.

PLANT PROFILE

HEIGHT	2m (6ft)
SPREAD	1.2m (4ft)
TYPE	Old garden rose
HARDINESS	Fully hardy
FLOWERING	Summer to autumn

M | 'Madame Plantier'

THE EXPERTS MIGHT QUIBBLE over whether this rose is in the Alba or the Noisette group, but the key point is that it can be a large, arching shrub, studded with creamy-white flowers, or a climber, spreading to 6m (20ft) across when given support. The flowers are like small pompoms, flat on top, and the grey-green stems (the same colour as the leaves) have few thorns. To prune for a shrub, remove only diseased, dead, and damaged growth, and trim for shape in late winter. Harder pruning results in fewer stems with larger flowers, while lighter pruning gives more stems with smaller blooms.

PLANT PROFILE

HEIGHT 2m (6ft)

SPREAD 2.5m (8ft)

TYPE Old garden rose

HARDINESS Fully hardy

FLOWERING Midsummer

'Maiden's Blush'

M

SOMETIMES KNOWN AS 'GREAT MAIDEN'S BLUSH', this Alba rose has a free-and-easy look in midsummer, when there is a lovely show of pale pink, lightly scented flowers. It adds a gentle touch to cottage gardens with its blue-grey leaves, and can be incorporated in a mixed rose hedge. The French call it 'Cuisse de Nymphe', which means the thigh of the nymph, referring to its fresh, skin-pink colour. Remove only diseased, dead, and damaged growth, and prune lightly for shape. Harder pruning will produce fewer stems with larger flowers.

PLANT PROFILE	
HEIGHT	1.5m (5ft)
SPREAD	1.2m (4ft)
TYPE	Old garden rose
HARDINESS	Fully hardy
FLOWERING	Midsummer

M

'Maigold'

ITS EARLY-FLOWERING, HYBRID NATURE – bigger than a shrub, shorter than a typical climber – and profusion of buff-yellow flowers make 'Maigold' extremely popular. Add to that a few later flowers, the healthy, glossy foliage and a lovely rich scent, and it is obvious why it has been a big hit since 1953. But beware of the thorny stems and note that there are no repeat flowers. There is no need to prune for the first two years, but do train new shoots into a horizontal position. From then on prune in the autumn, after flowering, nipping back the main stems and shortening sideshoots by two-thirds.

PLANT PROFILE

HEIGHT 2.5m (8ft)

TYPE Climber

HARDINESS Fully hardy

FLOWERING Early summer and autumn

MANY HAPPY RETURNS ('Harwanted')

M

IT'S NOT JUST THE NAME that has made this rose such a big hit (it won a clutch of awards in the 1980s), but also its prolific show of blush-pink flowers all summer on the spreading, bushy, disease-free growth. The shiny foliage is equally attractive, giving an all-over, healthy look. The autumn show of hips is a big bonus. MANY HAPPY RETURNS is well worth growing towards the front of a border or even in a large tub. In late winter cut back the main stems to 25–45cm (10–18in) above the ground, and reduce sideshoots by about one-third of their length.

PLANT PROFILE

HEIGHT 75cm (30in)

SPREAD 75cm (30in)

TYPE Bush (cluster-flowered)

HARDINESS Fully hardy

FLOWERING Summer to autumn; hips in autumn

M | 'Marchesa Boccella'

ONE OF THE PORTLAND GROUP OF ROSES, characterized by
healthy growth and strong scent, 'Marchesa Boccella' is big and
upright enough to make a small hedge. It has strong, thorny
growth, foliage that turns greyish-green, and clusters of
scented, rose-pink flowers. The rose sold as 'Jacques Cartier' is
reckoned to be exactly the same. Prune stems in late winter by
one-half to two-thirds. Harder pruning gives fewer stems with
larger flowers, while lighter pruning gives more flowering
stems with slightly smaller blooms.

PLANT PROFILE

HEIGHT	1.2m (4ft)
SPREAD	90cm (3ft)
TYPE	Old garden rose
HARDINESS	Fully hardy
FLOWERING	Summer to autumn

'Maréchal Niel'

M

THIS IS ONE FOR THE SPECIALIST because it is not totally hardy and the flowers do not stand up well to the rain. But give it a sunny, sheltered, modest-sized wall, and you can see why the French could not wait to get their hands on it when it was introduced in the mid-19th century. The large, high-pointed flowers are golden-yellow with a sweet scent. For the first two years train new shoots into a horizontal position to produce flowering sideshoots. From then on prune in the autumn, after flowering, nipping back the main stems and shortening sideshoots by two-thirds.

PLANT PROFILE
HEIGHT To 5m (15ft)
TYPE Climber
HARDINESS Fully hardy (borderline)
FLOWERING Summer to autumn

M | MARGARET MERRIL ('Harkuly')

A FIRST-RATE, PALE PINK-WHITE ROSE, it is beautifully shaped and has sweet-scented flowers of 28 petals, each bloom being 10cm (4in) wide. The flowers are perfectly set off by the crisp, dark green leaves. Though rather on the short side, MARGARET MERRIL has attractive, bushy growth and, since being introduced in 1977, has been a big success, winning many awards, including three for fragrance. In late winter prune back the main stems to approximately 25–45cm (10–18in) above the ground, and reduce sideshoots by one-third of their length.

PLANT PROFILE

HEIGHT 80cm (32in)

SPREAD 60cm (24in)

TYPE Bush (cluster-flowered)

HARDINESS Fully hardy

FLOWERING Summer to autumn

'Marguerite Hilling'

M

GROWTH IS VIGOROUS AND ARCHING, and incredibly flowery. After the main burst of rose-pink flowers there are more blooms intermittently in the autumn, given good weather. 'Marguerite Hilling' also makes a very good hedge. Remove all dead, diseased, and damaged growth and prune the remaining stems quite hard in late winter to promote plenty of new, vigorous, flowering shoots.

PLANT PROFILE
HEIGHT 2.2m (7ft)
SPREAD 2.2m (7ft)
TYPE Shrub
HARDINESS Fully hardy
FLOWERING Early summer and autumn

M | MARY ROSE ('Ausmary')

WITH AN ABUNDANCE OF FLOWERS with old-world charm,
MARY ROSE is ideal for cottage gardens. It is repeat-flowering
and its blooms have a light, barely discernible scent. The
flowers will not win any prizes on the show bench, but cannot
be faulted as part of a general garden scheme. Growth is
twiggy, bushy, and uneven, and perfectly disease-resistant.
MARY ROSE was introduced in 1983 to celebrate the salvage
of Henry VIII's flagship in Hampshire. In late winter, remove
dead, diseased, and damaged growth, leaving the old wood
intact. Trim for shape at the same time if necessary.

PLANT PROFILE

HEIGHT 1.2m (4ft)

SPREAD 1m (3ft)

TYPE Shrub

HARDINESS Fully hardy

FLOWERING Summer to autumn

'Max Graf'

M

A VALUABLE GROUND-COVER ROSE, 'Max Graf' (also called
R. x jacksonii 'Max Graf') makes thick, weed-suppressing
growth that roots as it extends. Let it grow freely across a bank
or tumble over a wall, but beware the thorns when weeding
close by. The flowers have a fresh apple-like scent and appear
in one burst that lasts a long time either side of midsummer.
Once it has taken up all the available space, prune it back in
late winter to outward-facing buds and keep an eye on it in
case it takes off again. Sideshoots can also be shortened at the
same time if necessary.

PLANT PROFILE	
HEIGHT 1.2m (4ft)	
SPREAD 3m (10ft) or more	
TYPE Ground-cover	
HARDINESS Fully hardy	
FLOWERING Midsummer	

M | 'Mermaid'

A GIANT OF A CLIMBER (even on cold, shady walls), 'Mermaid' has bright yellow, lightly scented flowers that continue through the second half of summer. It is disease-resistant and healthy, and prefers a sheltered, sunny wall. Also, it can be slow to put on growth initially, but the wait (given good conditions) is worth it. Avoid pruning for the first two years, but train new shoots into a horizontal position. From the third year prune in the autumn, after flowering, nipping back overlong main stems, and shortening sideshoots by two-thirds.

PLANT PROFILE	
HEIGHT To 6m (20ft)	
TYPE Climber	
HARDINESS Fully hardy	
FLOWERING Summer to autumn	

'Moonlight'

M

BUSHY AND STRONG ENOUGH to make a good hedge, 'Moonlight' has dark, glossy foliage that sets off the creamy buds. The buds gradually turn to white, with a touch of yellow in the centre. They appear in wonderfully impressive sprays and there is extra colour from the reddish–green stems. Though traditionally grown as a 1.2m (4ft) high shrub, it can double that figure if encouraged to spread or climb. When pruning remove only diseased, dead, and damaged growth. A minimal late-winter prune helps create a balanced shape, while harder pruning gives fewer stems with larger flowers.

PLANT PROFILE

HEIGHT	1.2m (4ft)
SPREAD	1.2m (4ft)
TYPE	Shrub
HARDINESS	Fully hardy
FLOWERING	Summer to autumn

M | 'Morning Jewel'

A USEFUL, MODEST CLIMBER, 'Morning Jewel' is happy in partial shade or full sun, and is ideal for pillars and pergola posts because it is not uncontrollably rampant. The leaves add to the show because they are healthily glossy, and the scented, bright pink flowers keep appearing all summer. It scores high points in every respect and will not let you down. It is often listed as a hybrid musk. For the first two years train new shoots into a horizontal position to yield flowering sideshoots. From then on prune in the autumn, after flowering, trimming the main stems if necessary and sideshoots by two-thirds.

PLANT PROFILE

HEIGHT 3m (10ft)

TYPE Climber

HARDINESS Fully hardy

FLOWERING Summer to autumn

moschata Musk rose

M

SOMETIMES CALLED A SMALL CLIMBER (or rambler), or tall
shrub, the most important thing about this rose is that the
flowers do not appear until late summer, and that is why it is
grown. They bloom in a beautiful show of open, scented,
creamy-white sprays, with purplish-green leaves, which carries
on into autumn. *R. moschata* was rediscovered in the early
1960s (having first appeared in the 16th century), and adds a
relaxed touch in cottage gardens. Leave the fading flowers
uncut and you will get plenty of orange-red hips. Minimal
pruning is required.

PLANT PROFILE	
HEIGHT To 3m (10ft)	
SPREAD To 3m (10ft)	
TYPE Wild	
HARDINESS Frost hardy	
FLOWERING Late summer to autumn; hips in autumn	

M | MOUNTBATTEN ('Harmantelle')

VIGOROUS, TALL, AND SHRUBBY with a good covering of large, dark green leaves, MOUNTBATTEN is not typical of the cluster-flowered bush roses. Its first batch of flowers is very impressive – they are about 10cm (4in) wide and cupped, on long stems – with many more after, as you would expect from a rose that has received several awards and medals. A failsafe choice for a novice gardener. In late winter cut back the main stems to 25–45cm (10–18in) long, and reduce the sideshoots by two-thirds of their length.

PLANT PROFILE

HEIGHT 1.2m (4ft)

SPREAD 75cm (30in)

TYPE Bush (cluster-flowered)

HARDINESS Fully hardy

FLOWERING Summer to autumn

moyesii 'Geranium'

M

THIS ROSE HAS BRIGHT, CHERRY-RED FLOWERS followed by superb, large red hips in late summer, and lovely, bright green leaves. Its parent, *R. moyesii*, is a giant, at 4m (12ft) high and 3m (10ft) wide, with scarlet flowers and red hips, so unless you have a huge garden, *R. moyesii* 'Geranium' is the one to go for. Remove only diseased, dead, and damaged growth in late winter, and give a general trim for a balanced shape.

PLANT PROFILE
HEIGHT 2.5m (8ft)
SPREAD 1.5m (5ft)
TYPE Shrub
HARDINESS Fully hardy
FLOWERING Summer; hips in late summer

M | 'Mrs John Laing'

THE ROUNDED, CUPPED FLOWERS contain tightly packed
petals, and have a lovely, strong scent. The colour is more
silvery-pink with a hint of lilac than plain pink, giving an
added attraction, while the virtually thorn-free stems make it
an easy rose to weed round. It grows well, even in poor soil,
and adds a gentle hue to pastel-coloured schemes. In formal
gardens prune shoots by one-half to two-thirds in late winter.
In less formal and cottage gardens remove only diseased, dead,
and damaged growth, and give a light overall prune for shape.

PLANT PROFILE

HEIGHT 90cm (3ft)

SPREAD 75cm (30in)

TYPE Old garden rose

HARDINESS Fully hardy

FLOWERING Summer to autumn

'Mrs Oakley Fisher'

M

SINCE BEING INTRODUCED IN 1921, 'Mrs Oakley Fisher' has been highly regarded by rose experts for its slightly unusual, highly scented flowers. The flowers are flat and 8cm (3in) wide, combining orange and yellow on spindly stems with sparse, bronze-green foliage. The flower colour eventually fades to pale buff. In late winter, remove all unproductive stems, and prune the remainder hard to outward-facing buds at 20–25cm (8–10in) above ground. This helps remove crisscrossing shoots in the centre of the bush. For larger, showier flowers prune harder, leaving just two or three buds.

PLANT PROFILE	
HEIGHT To 90cm (3ft)	
SPREAD To 90cm (3ft)	
TYPE Bush (large-flowered)	
HARDINESS Fully hardy	
FLOWERING Summer to autumn	

M | *mulliganii*

A MASSIVE, RAMPANT ROSE, *R. mulliganii* is an incredibly vigorous wild rambler and needs careful siting. A strong host tree is needed to support its growth, which hangs on with hooked thorns. There is a profusion of small flower clusters, plus a fruity scent and glossy, dark green leaves. Added colour comes from the reddish new shoots, the creamy buds, and the orange-red hips. The overall impact is hugely impressive. In late summer, for the first two years, prune sideshoots by 8cm (3in) to a strong new shoot. From then on prune up to one-third of the oldest main stems to ground level.

PLANT PROFILE
HEIGHT To 6m (20ft)
TYPE Rambler
HARDINESS Fully hardy
FLOWERING Midsummer; hips in autumn

'National Trust'

WITH EXQUISITE FLOWERS that withstand bad weather and sit smartly upright on strong stems against dark green leaves, this rose is a winner, apart from its lack of scent. Its small size means it is easy to find room for it at the front of a border, or in a mixed rose scheme. It makes good gift for anyone who thinks such roses do not belong in contemporary gardens. Prune in late winter, removing unproductive stems, and cut back the remainder hard to outward-facing buds 20–25cm (8–10in) above the ground. For large, showy flowers prune harder, leaving just two or three buds.

N

PLANT PROFILE	
HEIGHT 60cm (24in)	
SPREAD 60cm (24in)	
TYPE Bush (large-flowered)	
HARDINESS Fully hardy	
FLOWERING Summer to autumn	

N | 'Nevada'

ON A HOT, SUNNY DAY before midsummer 'Nevada' is
absolutely packed with flowers and there are few roses to rival
it. Each flower is about 10cm (4in) wide and the stems, before
they are obscured, are reddish-brown. After the main burst of
flowers there are more blooms, intermittently, in the autumn,
given good weather. 'Nevada' also makes a very good hedge.
Prune by removing only diseased, dead, and damaged growth,
leaving the old wood intact. Give a trim in late winter to help
produce a balanced shape; harder pruning gives fewer stems
with larger flowers.

PLANT PROFILE

HEIGHT 2.2m (7ft)

SPREAD 2.2m (7ft)

TYPE Shrub

HARDINESS Fully hardy

FLOWERING Early summer and
sparsely in autumn

'New Dawn'

A BIG HIT when it was introduced in 1930, 'New Dawn' remains a big seller for three reasons: the pale, pearl-pink, scented flowers keep opening in clusters from midsummer after the initial burst, the growth is reasonably restrained, and the leaves are attractively glossy. Also, it can be trained into trees, grown as a large bush, or incorporated in a hedge. It even grows on cold, shady walls. In the first two years train new shoots into a horizontal position. From then on prune in the autumn, after flowering, nipping back any overlong main stems and shortening sideshoots by two-thirds.

PLANT PROFILE

HEIGHT 3m (10ft)

TYPE Climber

HARDINESS Fully hardy

FLOWERING Summer to autumn

N | NICE DAY ('Chewsea')

A MINIATURE CLIMBER, this is just what you need where space is extremely limited. The small, scented flowers (which are shaped like a rosette) are a lovely mix of salmon, orange, and pink, and the buds keep opening in clusters over the summer months. Miniature climbers went on sale in 1990 in the UK. If you have a go at trying to prune them to restrict height, the plants respond by putting up more climbing shoots from the base, where you don't want them, making the rose bushier. In other words, when it comes to pruning, don't.

PLANT PROFILE

HEIGHT 2m (6ft)

TYPE Climber

HARDINESS Fully hardy

FLOWERING Summer

'Noisette Carnée'

SOMETIMES CALLED 'BLUSH NOISETTE', this is a dual-purpose Noisette rose. It can either be trained against a sunny, sheltered wall, growing to 4m (12ft), or be allowed to mound at the back of a border, where it makes a large shrub 2m (6ft) high. It may not be an all-time favourite, but it does have dark pink buds and repeat-flowers well and, with its old-fashioned look, is ideal for the cottage garden. For a climber, train new shoots horizontally for the first two years. Then prune in the autumn, trimming the main stems, and shortening sideshoots by two-thirds. For a shrub, remove dead, diseased, and damaged wood.

PLANT PROFILE

HEIGHT 2–4m (6–12ft)

TYPE Climber

HARDINESS Fully hardy

FLOWERING Summer to autumn

N | NORFOLK ('Poulfolk')

COVERING A SMALL AREA with scented, yellow flowers, this is not exactly the widest-spreading ground-cover rose available but, with dense growth, it keeps down weeds, and does the job very well. The leaves are healthy, glossy green, which compensates for the sporadic show of flowers after the main burst. NORFOLK can also be grown in tubs and large pots. Minimal pruning is required, but if growth is getting too rampant cut back to an outward-facing bud in late winter. Shorten sideshoots at the same time if necessary.

PLANT PROFILE

HEIGHT 75cm (30in)

SPREAD 90cm (3ft)

TYPE Ground-cover

HARDINESS Fully hardy

FLOWERING Summer

'Nozomi'

A GROUND-COVER ROSE with a difference, 'Nozomi' can also be trained and encouraged to grow up a post on a pergola, or a short pillar, to a height of about 1.5m (5ft). Either way, it makes trailing growth covered by glossy, dark green leaves and clusters of barely scented, small, pale pink-white flowers in summer. Because it flowers on the previous year's wood, prune it lightly or you will remove all this year's flower buds and end up with a shapely plant but hardly any flowers. Be restrained.

PLANT PROFILE

HEIGHT 45cm (18in)

SPREAD 1.2m (4ft)

TYPE Ground-cover

HARDINESS Fully hardy

FLOWERING Summer

N | *nutkana* 'Plena'

IN SOME REFERENCE BOOKS this rose goes under its old name of *R. californica* 'Plena'. You are likely to find it only in specialist nurseries, which is a shame because it is a terrific, leafy shrub. The sprays of rich pink flowers, with yellow stamens in the centre, appear on the arching, reddish-brown wood that has sharp grey thorns. It grows to quite a size, and looks best in cottage gardens and hedges. To create a large shrub remove only diseased, dead, and damaged growth. Harder pruning gives fewer stems with larger flowers, and lighter pruning more stems but smaller blooms.

PLANT PROFILE

HEIGHT 1.5–2.5m (5–8ft)

SPREAD 1.2–2m (4–6ft)

TYPE Wild

HARDINESS Fully hardy

FLOWERING Midsummer

x *odorata* 'Mutabilis'

O

THIS SPECTACULAR CHINA ROSE needs a sunny, sheltered position. In mild weather it starts flowering in late spring, and after its main flower burst in early summer new buds keep appearing, never with quite the same intensity, but always adding plenty of colour. Growth is twiggy and open, and long, lax stems may need support. Even before it starts flowering, it is beautifully coloured with plum-red new stems and fluttering leaves. The flowers open copper-yellow, changing to pink then copper-crimson before falling. Against a wall, it will climb to 3m (10ft). Give a light late-winter trim for shape.

PLANT PROFILE	
HEIGHT	2m (6ft)
SPREAD	2m (6ft)
TYPE	Old garden rose
HARDINESS	Fully hardy
FLOWERING	Late spring to autumn

O x *odorata* 'Viridiflora' Green rose

A BIZARRE CHIINA ROSE, which you will not find in any parks or bedding schemes, it has promising bluish-green buds that open to reveal clusters of small green petals, resembling leaves, which soon acquire a purplish-brown colour. It is more likely to elicit a "What's that?" than a "Where can I get one?", but if you fancy something very different, this is one to try. In late winter prune shoots by one-half to two-thirds. The harder you prune, the fewer the stems and the larger the flowers, while lighter pruning gives more stems with smaller blooms.

PLANT PROFILE	
HEIGHT	75cm (30in)
SPREAD	75cm (30in)
TYPE	Old garden rose
HARDINESS	Fully hardy
FLOWERING	Summer to autumn

ORANGES AND LEMONS ('Macoranlem')

In the right scheme, the upright Oranges and Lemons is a big plus. The flowers are a strange mishmash of an orange-yellow background and scarlet (fading to pinkish-red) stripes, speckles, and blotches. The first reaction is either a definite "yes", or a "not in my garden". Its glossy, dark green leaves are nicely coloured with a red tinge when they are young. In late winter cut back the main stems to 25–45cm (10–18in) above the ground, and shorten sideshoots by about one-third.

O

PLANT PROFILE	
HEIGHT	80cm (32in)
SPREAD	60cm (24in)
TYPE	Bush (cluster-flowered)
HARDINESS	Fully hardy
FLOWERING	Summer to autumn

P | PARTRIDGE ('Korweirim')

THIS IS ONE OF THE WIDEST-SPREADING ground-cover roses and it definitely needs a lot of space. For that reason it can also be grown over banks and tumbling over a wall, and it makes nice, rampant edging along the side of an artificial pond. Unlike many ground-cover roses, PARTRIDGE also has a strong scent. Minimal pruning is required, but if growth is getting too rampant cut it back to an outward-facing bud in late winter. Sideshoots can also be shortened then if necessary. Don't expect to keep it small, though.

PLANT PROFILE

HEIGHT 75cm (30in)

SPREAD 3m (10ft)

TYPE Ground-cover

HARDINESS Fully hardy

FLOWERING Mid- and late summer

'Paul Neyron'

THE BEST REASONS FOR GROWING this Hybrid Perpetual rose
are the enormous, 15cm (6in) wide flowers, with ruffled, lilac-
tinged, deep pink petals (without a strong scent to match).
From a distance they look like peonies and, while some dislike
their extravagance, 'Paul Neyron' does provide wonderful cut
flowers and a blowsy touch for cottage gardens. Growth is
vigorous and upright. In formal gardens prune shoots by one-
half to two-thirds in late winter. In less formal and cottage
gardens remove only diseased, dead, and damaged growth, and
give a light overall prune for shape.

PLANT PROFILE	
HEIGHT 1.5m (5ft)	
SPREAD 1.2m (4ft)	
TYPE Old garden rose	
HARDINESS Fully hardy	
FLOWERING Summer to autumn	

P | PAUL SHIRVILLE ('Harqueterwife')

AN EXQUISITE ROSE, the colour is hard to pin down and is much more than plain pink; there are hints of rosy-salmon, and possibly peach. It is well worth its place to the front of a pastel border, while the flowers perk up cut-flower displays. The first batch of scented flowers has a high centre, though subsequent blooms might not be quite as good. In late winter remove unproductive stems and prune the rest to outward-facing buds at 20–25cm (8–10in). This helps remove crisscrossing shoots in the centre of the bush. For large, showy flowers prune harder, to two or three buds.

PLANT PROFILE

HEIGHT 90cm (3ft)

SPREAD 75cm (30in)

TYPE Bush (large-flowered)

HARDINESS Fully hardy

FLOWERING Summer to autumn

'Paul's Himalayan Musk'

THE LONG, THIN STEMS need training up into a tree, where they shoot out arching, prickly growth. Then, just before midsummer, hundreds of sprays of tiny buds appear. Each flower is small and insignificant, but when every bud is open the tree turns into a fantastic whoosh of pale pink. There is only one show of flowers, but it is terrific. In late summer, for the first two years, prune sideshoots by 8cm (3in) to a strong new shoot. From the third year prune up to one-third of the oldest main stems to ground level.

PLANT PROFILE	
HEIGHT	10m (30ft)
TYPE	Rambler
HARDINESS	Fully hardy
FLOWERING	Midsummer

P

P

'Paul's Lemon Pillar'

NOT THE BIGGEST CLIMBER, but the once-only show of flowers does come just before midsummer, with a gentle citrus scent. The 12cm (5in) wide, high-pointed flowers are beautifully shaped, on stiff, upright stems that can be trained round a pillar or the post of a pergola. Provide adjacent climbers to flower before and afterwards, and you have got a first-rate show. For the first two years train new shoots into a horizontal position to produce flowering sideshoots. Then prune regularly in the autumn, nipping back the main stems if necessary and shortening sideshoots by two-thirds.

PLANT PROFILE

HEIGHT 4m (12ft)

TYPE Climber

HARDINESS Fully hardy

FLOWERING Summer

'Paul's Scarlet Climber'

P

THE BREAKING OPEN OF THE BUDS and the great show of scarlet flowers is a good way to start summer. As the only climbing rose in the garden, it does not have that much to offer as it is not scented, and there is just one show of flowers, but in combination with others (flowering before and after), it is a good, striking choice. It is sometimes listed in catalogues as a rambler. Avoid pruning for the first two years, but train new shoots into a horizontal position for flowering sideshoots. Prune in the autumn from the third year, nipping back overlong main stems and shortening sideshoots by two-thirds.

PLANT PROFILE	
HEIGHT 3m (10ft)	
TYPE Climber	
HARDINESS Fully hardy	
FLOWERING Early summer	

P

PEACE ('Madame A. Meilland')

THE PINK-TINGED, YELLOW PEACE was once one of the biggest names in the rose world. There has been a bit of a backlash due to overkill and snobbery, but it remains a fine choice. Growth is shrubby and vigorous, with glossy, dark green foliage, and the flowers are heavy and 15cm (6in) across but lack scent. It is a good choice for the non-green-fingered, requiring little pruning. In late winter remove all unproductive stems, and prune the rest to outward-facing buds at 20–25cm (8–10in). This helps remove crossing shoots in the centre. For large, showy flowers prune harder, to just two or three buds.

PLANT PROFILE

HEIGHT 1.2m (4ft)

SPREAD 90cm (3ft)

TYPE Bush (large-flowered)

HARDINESS Fully hardy

FLOWERING Summer to autumn

PEARL DRIFT ('Leggab')

EQUALLY GOOD AS A SHRUB or a low, dense hedge, this rose has a good covering of large, glossy, dark green leaves. The flowers are on the cottage-garden side, being flat and open with yellow stamens rather than sophisticated and shapely, and they repeat-flower over summer. PEARL DRIFT has an easy-going, relaxed feel. Some rose growers detect a hint of pink in the flowers, but if so it is very subtle. Remove only diseased, dead, and damaged growth when pruning. A minimal late-winter prune also yields a balanced shape. Harder pruning gives fewer stems with larger flowers, and lighter pruning the reverse.

PLANT PROFILE	
HEIGHT	90cm (3ft)
SPREAD	1.2m (4ft)
TYPE	Shrub
HARDINESS	Fully hardy
FLOWERING	Summer to autumn

P | 'Penelope'

WONDERFUL SPRAYS OF SALMON-PINK BUDS and creamy-pink flowers last over the summer, more creamy than pink in full sun, followed by hips. Initially green, the hips soon turn reddish-pink. Prune it and it stays small, but untouched it will reach 2m (6ft) tall and wide. Rose experts get carried away when describing 'Penelope', and there is no doubt that the unpruned version makes a strong impression. Remove only diseased, dead, and damaged growth, and leave the old wood. A minimal prune in late winter also yields a balanced shape. If required, harder pruning gives fewer stems with larger flowers.

PLANT PROFILE

HEIGHT 1.1m (3½ft)

SPREAD 1.1m (3½ft)

TYPE Shrub

HARDINESS Fully hardy

FLOWERING Summer to autumn; hips in autumn

PENNY LANE ('Hardwell')

IN 1998 IT WAS VOTED ROSE OF THE YEAR in the UK, the first climber to gain that honour. PENNY LANE combines the charm of an old garden rose with a continuous supply of flowers over summer on stiff stems with healthy, dark green leaves. The light honey-coloured flowers slowly turn pale pink. It is ideal in cottage gardens, growing up a pergola or over an arch, and adds a calming touch to brighter colours. In the first two years train new shoots horizontally. From the third year prune in the autumn, nipping back overlong main stems, and shortening sideshoots by two-thirds.

P

PLANT PROFILE

HEIGHT 4m (12ft)

TYPE Climber

HARDINESS Fully hardy

FLOWERING Summer

P

'Perle d'Or'

SCORING HIGH POINTS for its lovely scent, this China rose also has a covering of yellowish-orange, urn-shaped buds that open to reveal pale apricot-coloured flowers, which turn creamy with age, set against dark green leaves. Growth is twiggy and spindly. The translation of the name means golden pearl, which reflects the plant raiser's aim rather than the reality. In late winter prune shoots by one-half to two-thirds, pruning harder for fewer stems with larger flowers, and more lightly for more flowering stems with slightly smaller blooms.

PLANT PROFILE

HEIGHT To 1.2m (4ft)

SPREAD 90cm (3ft)

TYPE Old garden rose

HARDINESS Fully hardy

FLOWERING Summer to autumn

'PHEASANT ('Kordapt')

P

ONE OF THE MOST IMPRESSIVE ground-cover roses, it has an immense spread and a repeat show of scented flowers, but do not think about growing it unless you have enough space. Good sites include a bank, or tumbling over a wall. The repeat-flowering is definitely a bonus, but the eventual size might well put many people off: this is a giant. Minimal pruning is needed, but if shoots are getting too rampant, cut them back to outward-facing buds in late winter, and shorten sideshoots. Do not hope to restrain it significantly by pruning.

PLANT PROFILE

HEIGHT	50cm (20in)
SPREAD	3m (10ft)
TYPE	Ground-cover
HARDINESS	Fully hardy
FLOWERING	Summer

P | 'Phyllis Bide'

OF THE CLIMBERS AND RAMBLERS that reach 2.5m (8ft) high, this might not have the strongest, richest colour (being yellow with a tinge of pale pink), but it probably gives the most immense covering with sprays of flowers. And that sweet-scented display keeps on, all summer, until the autumn, with small and dainty flowers and leaves. It is very impressive against walls and over pergolas. For the first two years avoid pruning, but train sideshoots horizontally. From then on, prune in the autumn, cutting back overlong main stems and shortening sideshoots by about two-thirds.

PLANT PROFILE

HEIGHT 2.5m (8ft)

TYPE Climber

HARDINESS Fully hardy

FLOWERING Summer to autumn

PICCADILLY ('Macar')

P

ONE OF THE BEST of the twin-coloured roses, PICCADILLY is red on top and yellow underneath, and what sounds like a gaudy combination is actually a blending, merging shading of the two colours. The faintly scented flowers are set against the reddish-green foliage, giving a high-quality rose that is hard to fault. In late winter remove all unproductive stems, and prune hard to outward-facing buds leaving 20–25cm (8–10in) of stem above ground. This helps remove crossing shoots in the centre of the bush. For large, showy flowers prune harder, to just two or three buds.

PLANT PROFILE	
HEIGHT	80cm (32in)
SPREAD	60cm (24in)
TYPE	Bush (large-flowered)
HARDINESS	Fully hardy
FLOWERING	Summer to autumn

P | *pimpinellifolia* 'Dunwich Rose'

TWO OF THESE ROSES, framing a large pot or special feature, add an effective cottage-garden touch. Growth is small, mounding, and free, with arching, prickly, wiry stems covered at the start of summer with pale lemon flowers followed by black hips. In the wild it grows on sandy coastal sites, sending plenty of new shoots out of the ground. If they spread too far, pull them off. The parent *R. pimpinellifolia* has white flowers. When pruning in late winter remove only diseased, dead, and damaged growth, and trim to produce a balanced shape.

PLANT PROFILE

HEIGHT 65cm (26in)

SPREAD 1.2m (4ft)

TYPE Shrub

HARDINESS Fully hardy

FLOWERING Early summer; hips in autumn

PINK BELLS ('Poulbells')

P

THE BELLS SERIES OFFERS SHORT, VERTICAL GROWTH and wide outward-spreading stems with glossy foliage and sprays of smallish, bright pink flowers. They appear in mid- and late summer, when the dense growth keeps down weeds. PINK BELLS cannot be packed into a small space, and is far too big for most borders. Use it on a spare patch of ground where the soil is not necessarily first-rate. Minimal pruning is required, but if growth is too rampant cut shoots back to outward-facing buds in late winter. Sideshoots can also be shortened then, but pruning will not restrain its vigorous spread.

PLANT PROFILE

HEIGHT	75cm (30in)
SPREAD	1.5m (5ft)
TYPE	Ground-cover
HARDINESS	Fully hardy
FLOWERING	Summer

P 'Pink Grootendorst'

NOT QUITE AS VIGOROUS AND LARGE as its crimson-red parent, 'F. J. Grootendorst', this rose has clusters of rose-pink blooms, which last well as cut flowers. It reliably flowers over summer, is disease-free, has upright, dense growth, and, with its coarse, dark green leaves, makes a perfectly decent cottage-garden hedge. A few specialist nurseries sell 'White Grootendorst', and both are usually listed as Rugosa roses in catalogues. In late winter prune shoots by one-half to two-thirds; harder pruning gives fewer stems with larger flowers, and lighter pruning more stems with smaller blooms.

PLANT PROFILE

HEIGHT 1.3m (4½ft)

SPREAD 1.1m (3½ft)

TYPE Shrub

HARDINESS Fully hardy

FLOWERING Summer to autumn

'Pink Perpétué'

IT MIGHT BE RESTRAINED IN HEIGHT, but not when it comes to repeat-flowering because the faintly scented pink blooms (richer pink beneath) keep appearing as late as autumn. Each flower is 8cm (3in) wide. Growth is easily trained up arches, pergolas, or even fences where you can take advantage of its wide-spreading habit. The leaves are leathery and dark green. For the first two years train new shoots into a horizontal position. From then on prune in the autumn, after flowering, nipping back the main stems if they are too long and shortening sideshoots by two-thirds.

PLANT PROFILE

HEIGHT To 3m (10ft)

TYPE Climber

HARDINESS Fully hardy

FLOWERING Summer to autumn

P

POLAR STAR ('Tanlarpost')

SOMETIMES KNOWN AS 'POLAR STERN', the UK Rose of the
Year in 1985 has a big garden presence. The large, white,
barely scented flowers are nearly 12cm (5in) wide, abundant,
and do not collapse in the rain. The growth stands tall and
upright. Some might find 'Polar Star' a bit too obvious, but it
is clearly very popular. In late winter remove the unproductive
stems and prune hard to outward-facing buds at 20–25cm
(8–10in) from the ground. Choosing an outward-facing bud
helps deter crossing shoots in the centre. For large, showy
flowers prune harder, to two or three buds.

PLANT PROFILE

HEIGHT 90cm (3ft)

SPREAD 70cm (28in)

TYPE Bush (large-flowered)

HARDINESS Fully hardy

FLOWERING Summer to autumn

POT O' GOLD ('Dicdivine')

P

PLANT PROFILE

THE BUDS SUGGEST HIGH-CENTRED FLOWERS but they actually end up attractively cupped. The fragrant, medium-size, golden-yellow flowers appear in large numbers (alone or in clusters) in summer and into autumn, withstanding rain and diseases. POT O' GOLD rarely disappoints in the border (especially in cottage gardens, where flower profusion is more important than perfectly shaped blooms), putting on vigorous, spreading growth. Prune in late winter, removing all unproductive stems, and cutting the rest to outward-facing buds at 20–25cm (8–10in). For large flowers prune harder, to two or three buds.

HEIGHT	75cm (30in)
SPREAD	60cm (24in)
TYPE	Bush (large-flowered)
HARDINESS	Fully hardy
FLOWERING	Summer to autumn

P

'Président de Sèze'

THIS MAKES A SPECIAL SIGHT for two reasons. First, the flowers have a wonderful two-tone colour, being rich magenta-crimson in the centre and lilac around the edge, which is even more surprising given that the buds are pink. Second, growth is strong with large leaves, making an attractive, open shape. A row of these Gallica roses makes a colourful summer divide, but they are not dense enough to make a conventional hedge. Remove only diseased, dead, and damaged growth, and give a light late-winter prune for a balanced shape. Harder pruning gives fewer stems with larger flowers.

PLANT PROFILE	
HEIGHT 1.2m (4ft)	
SPREAD 1.2m (4ft)	
TYPE Old garden rose	
HARDINESS Fully hardy	
FLOWERING Summer	

PRETTY POLLY ('Meitonje')

P

PRETTY POLLY IS ONE OF THE BEST of its kind. It is compact, bushy, and very vigorous, putting out a huge number of small flowers over summer. It is just right for a pot, or for edging the length of a path or the sides of a patio. The healthy-looking leaves are dark green. It may be hard to find in garden centres but is sold by specialist nurseries, sometimes being listed as a slightly taller patio rose. In late winter select the strongest shoots and remove all other growth. Cut the shoots back by approximately one-third to one-half. This regime forces up plenty of new, vigorous growth.

PLANT PROFILE
HEIGHT 40cm (16in)
SPREAD 45cm (18in)
TYPE Bush (cluster-flowered, miniature)
HARDINESS Fully hardy
FLOWERING Summer to autumn

P

'Prima Ballerina'

THE LOVELY RICH SCENT, beautiful shade of pink, and clearly visible, shapely flowers that stand up on strong necks compensate for the likelihood of mildew. 'Prima Ballerina' can be grown in groups of, say, three in a mixed border, or as one of the highlights in a pastel-coloured scheme. The pink petals are more rich and warm than pale and slight. Prune in late winter, removing all unproductive stems, and cut the rest hard to outward-facing buds at 20–25cm (8–10in). This helps remove crisscrossing shoots in the centre. For large, showy flowers prune harder, leaving just two or three buds.

PLANT PROFILE

HEIGHT 90cm (3ft)

SPREAD 60cm (24in)

TYPE Bush (large-flowered)

HARDINESS Fully hardy

FLOWERING Summer to autumn

primula Incense rose

THE SMELL (NOT QUITE LIKE INCENSE) actually comes from the young leaves, which have a slight grey tinge. The young stems are more colourful, being reddish-brown, while the flowers, emerging at the end of spring, tend to be pale primrose. They are followed by brownish-maroon-coloured hips. *R. primula* is a lovely, carefree sight with its almost arching, graceful stems and unobtrusive flowers. It makes a good start to the summer in cottage gardens. Remove only diseased, dead, and damaged growth. A minimal late-winter prune also helps produce a more balanced shape, if required.

PLANT PROFILE	
HEIGHT To 3m (10ft)	
SPREAD 2m (6ft)	
TYPE Wild	
HARDINESS Fully hardy (borderline)	
FLOWERING Late spring; hips in autumn	

P

'Pristine'

ON THE TALL AND THIN SIDE, 'Pristine' makes healthy, upright growth with large, dark green leaves and stands out in the border. It won a Royal National Rose Society medal for fragrance in 1973. The 12cm (5in) wide, shapely flowers are high-centred and well worth including in cut-flower displays. In the garden, the petals retain their pink colour without any fading. In late winter remove unproductive stems, and prune to outward-facing buds at 20–25cm (8–10in). For large, showy flowers prune harder to just two or three buds. You are aiming for an open-centred bush shape, with no crossing shoots.

PLANT PROFILE	
HEIGHT	1.2m (4ft)
SPREAD	75cm (30in)
TYPE	Bush (large-flowered)
HARDINESS	Fully hardy
FLOWERING	Summer to autumn

'Prosperity'

A LARGE SHRUB, 'Prosperity' has a profusion of light pink buds opening to creamy-white, nicely scented flowers, each 5cm (2in) wide. The dark green leaves provide a good background. It was introduced in 1919, and remains a high-class plant. 'Prosperity', and other hybrid musks with a similar multitude of smallish flowers, can be grown in large borders, though it can also be trained up against a wall. Remove diseased, dead, and damaged growth and give a minimal late-winter prune for a balanced shape. Harder pruning gives fewer stems with larger flowers, and lighter pruning more stems with smaller blooms.

PLANT PROFILE	
HEIGHT	2m (6ft)
SPREAD	1.2m (4ft)
TYPE	Shrub
HARDINESS	Fully hardy
FLOWERING	Summer to autumn

Q | QUEEN MOTHER ('Korquemu')

ON THE BORDERLINE between a patio and a slightly shorter miniature rose, QUEEN MOTHER (introduced to mark the 90th birthday of the late Queen Mother) has beautiful, soft pink flowers. They appear in large numbers on spreading, bushy growth, set against the glossy green foliage. It looks equally attractive in pots or the garden, where it can be used to edge paths or fill gaps. In late winter remove all growth apart from the strongest shoots, and cut them back by one-third to one-half. This regime forces up plenty of new, vigorous growth.

PLANT PROFILE

HEIGHT	40cm (16in)
SPREAD	60cm (24in)
TYPE	Bush (cluster-flowered, patio)
HARDINESS	Fully hardy
FLOWERING	Summer to autumn

'Rambling Rector'

IT PRODUCES A FANTASTIC SHOW of vigorous, arching stems with sweetly scented, small, open flowers with a yellow centre, followed by red hips. Grow it up into a substantial tree and its midsummer show will burst through the canopy in a mass of sprays. The prolific growth can easily cover an old shed or be incorporated into a hedgerow where the small thorns lock on to the host plant. In late summer, for the first two years, prune sideshoots by 8cm (3in) to a strong new shoot. From the third year prune at most one-third of the oldest main stems back to ground level.

PLANT PROFILE

HEIGHT 6m (20ft)

TYPE Rambler

HARDINESS Fully hardy

FLOWERING Summer; hips in autumn

R | 'Raubritter'

BECAUSE IT GROWS TWICE AS WIDE as it does vertically, some catalogues list 'Raubritter' as a ground-cover rose. It makes a large, sprawling, bushy mound with crisscrossing branches covered in dark green leaves and light pink flowers in a once-only midsummer display. It will certainly keep down weeds, but can also be grown to cover a bank or trail over a wall. Remove only diseased, dead, and damaged growth. A minimal late-winter prune also helps produce a balanced shape and more flowering stems with smaller blooms, while harder pruning gives fewer stems with larger flowers.

PLANT PROFILE

HEIGHT 90cm (3ft)

SPREAD 2m (6ft)

TYPE Shrub

HARDINESS Fully hardy

FLOWERING Midsummer

RED BLANKET ('Intercell')

R

HIGHLY EFFECTIVE AS GROUND COVER, 'Red Blanket' makes
spreading, bushy growth covered in a mass of dark green
leaves. The big features of the flowers are that the red pales to
white in the centre, and that the blooms appear in clusters
over a long period through summer. The possible likelihood of
black spot should not put you off. Little pruning is needed,
but if the growth is getting too rampant, cut it back to an
outward-facing bud in late winter. Sideshoots can also be
shortened at the same time if necessary.

PLANT PROFILE	
HEIGHT	75cm (30in)
SPREAD	1.2m (4ft)
TYPE	Ground-cover
HARDINESS	Fully hardy
FLOWERING	Summer to autumn

R | 'Reine des Violettes'

CLOSE TO AN OLD GARDEN ROSE in terms of flower shape and colour, 'Reine des Violettes' has the extra advantage of flowering well through summer, into autumn, on virtually thorn-free stems. The flowers are purple on opening before turning slightly paler and then lilac. It was introduced in 1860 and experts still put this Hybrid Perpetual high on their list of must-have roses. Pamper it with deep, rich soil. In formal gardens prune shoots by one-half to two-thirds in late winter. In less formal and cottage gardens remove only diseased, dead, and damaged growth, and give a light overall prune for shape.

PLANT PROFILE

HEIGHT 1.5m (5ft)

SPREAD 1.2m (4ft)

TYPE Old garden rose

HARDINESS Fully hardy

FLOWERING Summer to autumn

'Reine Victoria'

NAMED IN HONOUR OF QUEEN VICTORIA in 1872, this Bourbon rose is nothing like her forbidding, grey, huffy image. The flowers are beautifully cupped and rounded with 40 petals, being rich pink with a hint of mauve, on top of strong, erect, bushy growth. It exudes old-world charm, and is well worth including in a collection of old garden roses or at the back of a cottage-garden border. In late winter prune shoots by one-half to two-thirds. Harder pruning gives fewer stems with larger flowers, and lighter pruning more flowering stems with smaller blooms.

PLANT PROFILE	
HEIGHT 2m (6ft)	
SPREAD 1.2m (4ft)	
TYPE Old garden rose	
HARDINESS Fully hardy	
FLOWERING Summer to autumn	

R | REMEMBER ME ('Cocdestin')

OF ALL THE COPPER-COLOURED ROSES, this is one of the darkest. The flowers are nearly 10cm (4in) wide, appearing singly or in sprays on stiff, bushy growth. The leaves are glossy, dark green, creating an effective contrast. REMEMBER ME makes a nice addition to hothouse borders, combining well with reds and yellows, and keeps flowering into autumn. In late winter remove all unproductive stems, and prune the rest hard to outward-facing buds at 20–25cm (8–10in). This helps remove crisscrossing shoots in the centre of the bush. For large, showy flowers prune to just two or three buds.

PLANT PROFILE

HEIGHT 90cm (3ft)

SPREAD 60cm (24in)

TYPE Bush (large-flowered)

HARDINESS Fully hardy

FLOWERING Summer to autumn

ROBIN REDBREAST ('Interrob')

R

A MODEST GROUND-COVER ROSE compared to some of the vigorous wide-spreaders, ROBIN REDBREAST makes dense, bushy, thorny growth. The scentless, dark red flowers are small and open with a white eye, and are silver underneath. The leaves are glossy, dark green. It is a useful gap filler in borders, though it can also be grown in pots. ROBIN REDBREAST is not particularly widely sold, but is by no means hard to find. Minimal pruning is required, but if growth is getting too rampant, cut shoots back to outward-facing buds in late winter. Sideshoots can also be shortened then if necessary.

PLANT PROFILE	
HEIGHT	45cm (18in)
SPREAD	60cm (24in)
TYPE	Ground-cover
HARDINESS	Fully hardy
FLOWERING	Summer to autumn

R | 'Roger Lambelin'

GIVEN THE WONDERFUL COLOURING, with white edged, crimson-purple petals, and the lovely scent, this Hybrid Perpetual rose is definitely worth a try, but note that deep, rich soil is vital for good growth and a good display. Prepare it well before planting, and add well-rotted compost annually. It sometimes loses its white edges and reverts to red; if this happens there is nothing you can do to correct it. In formal gardens prune shoots by one-half to two-thirds in late winter. In less formal and cottage gardens remove only diseased, dead, and damaged growth, and give a light overall prune for shape.

PLANT PROFILE

HEIGHT	90cm (3ft)
SPREAD	90cm (3ft)
TYPE	Old garden rose
HARDINESS	Fully hardy
FLOWERING	Summer to autumn

ROSE GAUJARD ('Gaumo')

R

A GOOD FUN ROSE, as popular now as when it was introduced in 1957, ROSE GAUJARD is a lively bush for perking up borders. With 80 petals, the flowers combine cherry-red above with pale pink and white beneath, while the leaves are large and glossy. Forget the virtual lack of scent; this keeps going without any let-up, and does not lose its colour. In late winter remove all unproductive stems, and prune the rest hard to outward-facing buds at 20–25cm (8–10in). Choosing a bud facing outwards helps remove and deter crossing central shoots. For large, showy flowers, prune to two or three buds.

PLANT PROFILE	
HEIGHT 90cm (3ft)	
SPREAD 75cm (30in)	
TYPE Bush (large-flowered)	
HARDINESS Fully hardy	
FLOWERING Summer to autumn	

R | ROSEMARY HARKNESS ('Harrowbord')

A FAILSAFE ORANGE with a touch of pink, ROSEMARY HARKNESS has a strong scent and good disease-resistance, with a reliable show of flowers all summer against bushy, branching, leafy growth. Being on the small side, under 90cm (3ft), it should be easy to slot into a gap in the border. It is a good contender for mixed rose schemes with either brash or quieter, pastel colours. Remove all unproductive stems in late winter, and prune the others hard to outward-facing buds at 20–25cm (8–10in). This helps maintain an open centre to the bush. For large, showy flowers prune to just two or three buds.

PLANT PROFILE	
HEIGHT 80cm (32in)	
SPREAD 80cm (32in)	
TYPE Bush (large-flowered)	
HARDINESS Fully hardy	
FLOWERING Summer to autumn	

'Roseraie de l'Haÿ'

R

A SUPERB SHRUB that has been a big hit for over 100 years, 'Roseraie de l'Haÿ' has enormous presence. Growth is so bushy and vigorous that it makes a very good hedge or feature at the back of a border. The buds are unusually long and attractive, being coloured wine-red. When open, the flowers are just over 10cm (4in) wide and rich purple-crimson with a strong scent. Even the leaves are a healthy, fresh green. Usually listed with the Rugosa roses in catalogues, it is excellent in every way. In late winter prune by one-half to two-thirds; pruning harder gives fewer stems with larger flowers.

PLANT PROFILE	
HEIGHT	2.2m (7ft)
SPREAD	2m (6ft)
TYPE	Shrub
HARDINESS	Fully hardy
FLOWERING	Summer to autumn

R | ROSY CUSHION ('Interall')

THIS MODERN SHRUB IS A GOOD CHOICE for two reasons.
First, it has pale pink, white-eyed, lightly scented flowers (and
the display really is continuous), and second, its dense mass of
prickly, leafy stems makes ground-covering, weed-suppressing
growth. It forms a large, bushy plant nicely softened by the
smallish, open flowers with seven or eight petals each. To
create an impressive shrub remove only diseased, dead, and
damaged growth. A light late-winter prune also helps produce
a balanced shape and results in more stems with smaller
blooms. Harder pruning gives fewer stems with larger flowers.

PLANT PROFILE	
HEIGHT	90cm (3ft)
SPREAD	1.2m (4ft)
TYPE	Shrub
HARDINESS	Fully hardy
FLOWERING	Summer to autumn

R

'Rosy Mantle'

THE SHAPELY, 10CM (4IN) WIDE FLOWERS of 'Rosy Mantle' are rose- to salmon-pink, appear in clusters, and have a very good scent. On the down side, its climbing stems are quite stiff and do not have that many leaves. For the first two years train the new shoots into a horizontal position to produce plenty of flowering sideshoots. From then on prune in the autumn, after flowering, nipping back the main stems if necessary and shortening the sideshoots by about two-thirds.

PLANT PROFILE
HEIGHT 2.5m (8ft)
TYPE Climber
HARDINESS Fully hardy
FLOWERING Summer to autumn

R *roxburghii* Burr rose, Chestnut rose, Chinquapin rose

THE ONE THING EVERYONE AGREES ON is that this is quirky, stiff-stemmed, colourful, and huge. It makes a robust, impenetrable shape thanks to the rigid growth and vicious prickles beneath the leaves, while the flowers are beautifully rounded and pinkish. They are followed by 2.5cm (1in) wide hips, said to look like small, green chestnuts, which gradually turn pale brown. Unlike most roses, it also looks good in winter because of its flaking, yellow-tinged bark. It is ideal for wild or cottage gardens. Remove only diseased, dead, and damaged growth and prune lightly for a balanced shape.

PLANT PROFILE
HEIGHT 2m (6ft)
SPREAD 2m (6ft)
TYPE Wild
HARDINESS Fully hardy
FLOWERING Summer; hips in autumn

ROYAL WILLIAM ('Korzaun')

R

THERE ARE SOME EXCELLENT CRIMSON-REDS among the large-flowered bush roses, and ROYAL WILLIAM is one of the best. It was voted UK Rose of the Year in 1987, and it is obvious why. The nicely shaped flowers do not get lost in any nearby summer mayhem thanks to their rich red colour and size, being 12cm (5in) wide. New buds keep appearing over summer, guaranteeing a good supply, and they are great for cutting. In late winter remove all unproductive stems, and prune the rest to outward facing buds at 20–25cm (8–10in). For large, showy flowers, prune to just two or three buds.

PLANT PROFILE
HEIGHT 90cm (3ft)
SPREAD 75cm (30in)
TYPE Bush (large-flowered)
HARDINESS Fully hardy
FLOWERING Summer to autumn

R | 'Ruby Wedding'

SOME EXPERTS CALL THIS "respectable", which mean that they do not rate it as a must-buy highly elegant rose, but it it is a perfectly decent red that will not let you down. Growth is bushy and spreading, and thanks to its smallish flowers (which some might call too small), 'Ruby Wedding' adds nicely to the flow in a border scheme where the appearance of the whole rates more highly than individual ingredients. In late winter remove all unproductive stems, and prune the rest hard to outward-facing buds at 20–25cm (8–10in) or, for large, showy flowers, prune harder to just two or three buds.

PLANT PROFILE

HEIGHT 90cm (3ft)

SPREAD 75cm (30in)

TYPE Bush (large-flowered)

HARDINESS Fully hardy

FLOWERING Summer

rugosa Hedgehog rose, Japanese rose, Ramanas rose   R

MORE ACCURATELY CALLED A WILD SHRUB ROSE, this rose has a range of good features. First, you can grow it in sandy soil and it certainly does not have to be pampered. Second, the dense, vigorous growth makes a thorny, impenetrable hedge with leathery, dark green leaves. Third, the scented flowers give a constant show over summer. Finally, they are followed by tomato-shaped, bright red hips, often with an orange tinge. In formal gardens prune shoots by one-half to two-thirds in late winter. In less formal and cottage gardens remove diseased, dead, and damaged growth, and give a light prune for shape.

PLANT PROFILE
HEIGHT 1–2.5m (3–8ft)
SPREAD 1–2.5m (3–8ft)
TYPE Shrub
HARDINESS Fully hardy
FLOWERING Summer to autumn; hips in autumn

R | *rugosa* 'Alba'

THE PURE WHITE VERSION of *R. rugosa*, this rose has silky flowers (opening from pinkish buds) right through the summer, which are promptly followed by an excellent show of large, shiny, orange-red hips. *R. rugosa* 'Alba' also has a good covering of bright green foliage and eventually makes a superb shrub. Prune it in late winter, after flowering, by one-half to two-thirds, though in cottage gardens and informal gardens pruning can be much lighter. In general, harder pruning gives fewer stems with larger flowers, and lighter pruning more flowering stems with smaller blooms.

PLANT PROFILE
HEIGHT 2m (6ft)
SPREAD 2m (6ft)
TYPE Shrub
HARDINESS Fully hardy
FLOWERING Summer to autumn; hips in autumn

'Salet'

OFTEN LISTED AS A MOSS ROSE, 'Salet' has light mossy growth on the stems and buds. The latter appear in clusters and open to clear pink, summer-long flowers. They have a ruffled, clustered arrangement of petals and exude an old-fashioned charm and a good scent. Introduced in France, in 1854, it is a good cottage-garden rose. To create a large shrub, remove only diseased, dead, and damaged growth, and leave the old wood intact. A light late-winter prune also helps produce a balanced shape and more flowering stems with smaller blooms, while harder pruning gives fewer stems with larger flowers.

PLANT PROFILE	
HEIGHT	1.2m (4ft)
SPREAD	90cm (3ft)
TYPE	Old garden rose
HARDINESS	Fully hardy
FLOWERING	Summer

S | 'Sally Holmes'

ATTRACTIVELY AND UNUSUALLY UPRIGHT, the highly distinctive 'Sally Holmes' sends up strong growth with clusters of scented, creamy-white flowers. Each one has five petals and lies open and flat, well clear of the glossy leaves. It has won a clutch of awards since being introduced in 1976, and is very popular. It is beautiful in cottage gardens. Remove only diseased, dead, and damaged growth when pruning. Give a minimal late-winter prune for a balanced shape if need be. Harder pruning gives fewer stems with larger flowers, and lighter pruning more flowering stems with smaller blooms.

PLANT PROFILE

HEIGHT	2m (6ft)
SPREAD	90cm (3ft)
TYPE	Shrub
HARDINESS	Fully hardy
FLOWERING	Summer to autumn

'Sander's White Rambler'

S

ITS BIG ASSET IS THE LATE SUMMER SHOW of smallish flowers in large clusters (when many other roses have stopped), with a fresh, fruity scent. It is excellent for making sure summer goes out on a high. Since being introduced in 1912, 'Sander's White Rambler' has been a big favourite, used in a wide range of ways. Grow it up pergolas, over arches, and into trees. In late summer, for the first two years, prune sideshoots by 8cm (3in) to a strong new shoot. From the third year prune at most one-third of the oldest main stems back to ground level.

PLANT PROFILE

HEIGHT 4m (12ft)

TYPE Rambler

HARDINESS Fully hardy

FLOWERING Late summer

S | 'Sarah van Fleet'

AS A THICK, THORNY, IMPENETRABLE, LEAFY HEDGE (keeping out people and animals) or a huge, upright shrub for the back of the border, this Rugosa rose is liberally covered with pink flowers, with just a hint of lilac. They start opening in early summer with their best show in midsummer, carrying on into autumn. The leaves can suffer from rust, and there are no hips. In formal gardens prune shoots by one-half to two-thirds in late winter. In less formal and cottage gardens remove only diseased, dead, and damaged growth, and give a light overall prune for shape.

PLANT PROFILE

HEIGHT	2.5m (8ft)
SPREAD	1.5m (5ft)
TYPE	Shrub
HARDINESS	Fully hardy
FLOWERING	Summer to autumn

SAVOY HOTEL ('Harvintage')

THE FLOWERS ARE BEAUTIFULLY SHAPED, the colour is soft, light pink, the growth is disease-free and bushy, and the leaves dark green. SAVOY HOTEL is an excellent, all-purpose small rose that gives a continuous supply of flowers over summer, and is ideal in mixed borders, with other roses, and as a cut flower. Introduced in 1989, it has won several top awards. In late winter remove all unproductive stems, and prune the rest hard to outward-facing buds at 20–25cm (8–10in). This helps remove crisscrossing shoots in the centre. For large, showy flowers prune harder, leaving just two or three buds.

PLANT PROFILE	
HEIGHT	80cm (32in)
SPREAD	60cm (24in)
TYPE	Bush (large-flowered)
HARDINESS	Fully hardy
FLOWERING	Summer to autumn

S

'Scabrosa'

MAKING AN IMPRESSIVELY DENSE, bushy, free-flowering, healthy hedge or shrub for the back of the border, 'Scabrosa' is a Rugosa rose highly rated for its ability to flower freely right through summer. Each bloom is 10cm (4in) wide or more, being followed by a good show of large, round, orange-red hips. It is sometimes listed as *R. rugosa* 'Scabrosa'. In formal gardens prune shoots by one-half to two-thirds in late winter. In less formal and cottage gardens remove only diseased, dead, and damaged growth, and give a light overall prune for shape.

PLANT PROFILE	
HEIGHT	1.7m (5½ft)
SPREAD	1.7m (5½ft)
TYPE	Shrub
HARDINESS	Fully hardy
FLOWERING	Summer to autumn; hips in autumn

'Scharlachglut'

S

ITS TRANSLATED NAME SCARLET FIRE (which is how it is often listed) gives a much clearer idea of what to expect from this rose: a midsummer blast of blazing, flashy scarlet flowers, each one 12cm (5in) wide with golden yellow in the middle, adding plenty of zip. The flowers are followed by large red hips. Though 'Scharlachglut' is used as a massive shrub it can be trained to grow up against a wall. To create a large, impressive shrub remove only diseased, dead, and damaged growth, and give a light prune in winter for shape. Harder pruning gives fewer stems with larger flowers.

PLANT PROFILE	
HEIGHT To 3m (10ft)	
SPREAD 2m (6ft)	
TYPE Shrub	
HARDINESS Fully hardy	
FLOWERING Summer; hips in autumn	

S

'Schoolgirl'

A SLIGHTLY QUIRKY NAME for this lanky, stiff-stemmed, branching climber. Its 10cm (4in) wide, shapely flowers are richly scented and look just as good after days of heavy rain. The deep apricot (nearly orange) colour is a boon since few other climbers have it, and the only minor fault is the sparseness of its leaves. It can be trained up any structure, from walls to pergolas. For the first two years, train new shoots into a horizontal position. From the third year, prune in the autumn, after flowering, nipping back the main stems if necessary, and shortening sideshoots by two-thirds.

PLANT PROFILE

HEIGHT 3m (10ft)

TYPE Climber

HARDINESS Fully hardy

FLOWERING Summer to autumn

'Seagull'

S

FIRING UP RAMPANT, ARCHING STEMS, 'Seagull' scrambles high into old, stout trees, where it produces large clusters of gold-centred small flowers, 2.5cm (1in) wide. It is irrelevant that the leaves are greyish-green because they mix in with those of the support tree. It can also be grown up pergolas and arches. In late summer, for the first two years, prune sideshoots by 8cm (3in) to a strong new shoot. From the third year prune at most one-third of the oldest main stems back to ground level.

PLANT PROFILE	
HEIGHT 6m (20ft)	
TYPE Rambler	
HARDINESS Fully hardy	
FLOWERING Summer	

S | *sericea* subsp. *omeiensis* f. *pteracantha* Winged thorn rose

FIRST, IGNORE THE IMPOSSIBLE NAME (most people just call it *R. pteracantha*) and second, look at one before you buy. This rose has the most fantastic, flattish-triangular thorns lined up along the stems, but they are vicious and not for gardens with children. The thorns can be 2cm (¾in) high and over 2.5cm (1in) wide at the base. Because they are reddish and translucent, make sure that the sun can shine through them. The few summer flowers are virtually irrelevant. A hard late-winter prune (to promote new growth) is vital because the thorns lose their colour in their second summer.

PLANT PROFILE

HEIGHT 2.5m (8ft)

SPREAD 2.2m (7ft)

TYPE Wild

HARDINESS Fully hardy

FLOWERING Summer

SEXY REXY ('Macrexy')

S

IT MIGHT SELL MORE ON ITS NAME than its flowers, but that does not stop them being very attractive. They are a gentle, soft pink and packed with petals on strong, healthy growth. The buds appear in large clusters. Make sure that you promptly snip off the fading flowers to promote even more to follow on. SEXY REXY makes a good gift because it is thoroughly reliable in every way. In late winter cut back the main stems to 25–45cm (10–18in) above the ground, and reduce sideshoots by about one-third of their length.

PLANT PROFILE	
HEIGHT 70cm (28in)	
SPREAD 60cm (24in)	
TYPE Bush (cluster-flowered)	
HARDINESS Fully hardy	
FLOWERING Summer to autumn	

S

SHARIFA ASMA ('Ausreef')

SHORT AND EXQUISITE, this 1989 introduction injects old-world charm into a repeat-flowering rose with soft pink flowers, paler pink at the edge. They are almost translucent, with a dash of yellow at the base. If that makes it sound a delicate plant, it is not – growth is quite vigorous, bushy, and compact. It makes a classy addition to formal and cottage gardens. In late winter prune shoots by one-half to two-thirds, pruning harder for fewer stems with larger flowers, and more lightly for more flowering stems with smaller blooms.

PLANT PROFILE

HEIGHT 90cm (3ft)

SPREAD 75cm (30in)

TYPE Shrub

HARDINESS Fully hardy

FLOWERING Summer

SHEILA'S PERFUME ('Harsherry') S

THE SECOND PART OF THE NAME is perfectly accurate. There is
a strong perfume (confirmed by two awards for fragrance),
though the colour may not be quite to everyone's liking. The
large, shapely flowers are yellow with red running unevenly
around the edges. The blooms appear individually or in
clusters set against the abundant, disease-resistant, glossy, dark
green leaves. Cut back the main stems in late winter to
25–45cm (10–18in), and reduce the sideshoots by about one-
third of their length.

PLANT PROFILE	
HEIGHT 75cm (30in)	
SPREAD 60cm (24in)	
TYPE Bush (cluster-flowered)	
HARDINESS Fully hardy	
FLOWERING Summer to autumn	

S   'Silver Jubilee'

NOT JUST A BEAUTIFUL MIX of three colours, pink, apricot–peach and cream (which do not fade), this rose also has petals perfectly arranged in symmetrical circles. There is a lovely scent, and the 12cm (5in) wide flowers keep appearing over summer. Growth is dense and leafy. Introduced in 1978, 'Silver Jubilee' later picked up four top rose awards. In late winter remove all unproductive stems, and prune the rest hard to outward-facing buds at 20–25cm (8–10in). This helps remove crisscrossing shoots in the centre. For large, showy flowers prune harder to just two or three buds.

PLANT PROFILE

HEIGHT	1.1m (3½ft)
SPREAD	60cm (24in)
TYPE	Bush (large-flowered)
HARDINESS	Fully hardy
FLOWERING	Summer to autumn

'Silver Wedding'

S

IT WILL CERTAINLY MAKE A GOOD GIFT, and this rose is far from being a novelty buy. The flowers have a nice symmetrical shape though with barely any scent, and appear in clusters over summer. The distinguishing feature of 'Silver Wedding' is its small size, being not far off a miniature rose. It can be grown in pots or tucked into a small gap in a border. In late winter remove all the unproductive stems, and prune the remainder to outward-facing buds, leaving 20–25cm (8–10in) of stem above the ground. For large, showy flowers prune harder to two or three buds.

PLANT PROFILE

HEIGHT 50cm (20in)

SPREAD 50cm (20in)

TYPE Bush (large-flowered)

HARDINESS Fully hardy

FLOWERING Summer to autumn

S | SIMBA ('Korbelma')

AN EXCELLENT ROSE FOR CUT FLOWERS, each large bloom is very stylish, with a high point. The flowers usually appear singly instead of in groups, withstand poor weather, and repeat through summer with a few gaps between each burst of buds. If you are buying it in Germany, it is called HELMUT SCHMIDT (after the ex-chancellor), the Americans call it GOLDSMITH, and the British name it after a dog, SIMBA. Remove all unproductive stems in late winter, and prune the remainder hard to outward-facing buds at 20–25cm (8–10in). For larger flowers prune harder, leaving just two or three buds.

PLANT PROFILE

HEIGHT 60cm (24in)

SPREAD 50cm (20in)

TYPE Bush (large-flowered)

HARDINESS Fully hardy

FLOWERING Summer to autumn

'Sombreuil'

THIS OLD-FASHIONED ROSE has blooms with a flat, crinkled, ruffled look, creamy-white with a dash of pale pink in the middle. There is a gorgeous sweet scent all summer from the continuous supply of flowers, while the leaves are lush green. Grow it against a sunny wall for the best effect. With pruning, 'Sombreuil' can become a shorter, dense, bushy shrub. To grow it as a climber, train new shoots into a horizontal position for the first two years. From then on prune in the autumn, after flowering, nipping back the main stems if they are too long, and shortening sideshoots by two-thirds.

PLANT PROFILE
HEIGHT 4m (12ft)
TYPE Climber
HARDINESS Fully hardy
FLOWERING Summer

S

'Southampton'

ITS RED-FLUSHED, APRICOT-ORANGE COLOUR, leafy bushiness, and the totally satisfying shape of the high-pointed flowers have made 'Southampton' very popular with the public and impressed the rose experts. The flowers are clearly on display all summer, appearing either individually or in clusters on firm stems, and provide good impact in a border. The glossy green foliage is disease-resistant. In late winter cut back the main stems to about 25–45cm (10–18in) above the ground, and reduce the sideshoots by about one-third of their length.

PLANT PROFILE

HEIGHT	1.1m (3½ft)
SPREAD	70cm (28in)
TYPE	Bush (cluster-flowered)
HARDINESS	Fully hardy
FLOWERING	Summer to autumn

'Souvenir de la Malmaison'

S

NAMED AFTER THE EMPRESS JOSEPHINE'S great French rose garden, this Bourbon rose lives up to its name. The large, 12cm (5in) wide flowers have the typical old garden rose, petal-packed, crumpled-ruffled look and deliver a lovely scent. Its repeat summer-flowering means it is quite capable of standing alone, in its own bed, on a lawn. It looks miserable after heavy rain, when the sodden flowers hang down, but that is only a brief hiccup. Some catalogues give its height and width as 90cm (3ft), but it will spread to 1.5m (5ft). In late winter prune shoots by one-half to two-thirds.

PLANT PROFILE

HEIGHT To 1.5m (5ft)

SPREAD To 1.5m (5ft)

TYPE Old garden rose

HARDINESS Fully hardy

FLOWERING Summer to autumn

S

'Souvenir de Saint Anne's'

CLOSELY RELATED TO 'SOUVENIR DE LA MALMAISON' (*see page 273*), many consider this rose slightly superior. The flowers are more shapely and do not get that hang-dog look after heavy rain, and they have a stronger scent, which apparently emanates from the stamens. It is also slightly more vigorous, taller, and bushier. A Bourbon rose, it was found growing in Ireland, near Dublin. In late winter prune the stems by one-half to two-thirds. Harder pruning gives fewer stems with larger flowers, while lighter pruning results in more flowering stems with slightly smaller blooms.

PLANT PROFILE

HEIGHT 1.5m (5ft)

SPREAD 1.5m (5ft)

TYPE Old garden rose

HARDINESS Fully hardy

FLOWERING Summer to autumn

'Souvenir du Docteur Jamain'

S

THE VELVETY PETALS are a deep, dark, wine red colour with just a hint of purple. To maintain this rich colour, keep it out of direct sun or the impact is lost, and the petals turn browny-red. The scent is strong and the first batch of flowers is the best. Dating back to to 1865, it is a sumptuous rose, with dark green leaves, and is well worth pampering. It can also be grown as a 3m (10ft) high wall climber. In formal gardens prune shoots by one-half to two-thirds in late winter. In less formal and cottage gardens remove only diseased, dead, and damaged growth, and give a light overall prune for shape.

PLANT PROFILE

HEIGHT 2m (6ft)

SPREAD 1.2m (4ft)

TYPE Old garden rose

HARDINESS Fully hardy

FLOWERING Midsummer and autumn

S 'Stanwell Perpetual'

FOUND BY ACCIDENT and introduced in 1838, this rose has been a big favourite in cottage gardens ever since. The pale pink flowers have an open shape and are loosely formed, appearing off-and-on over summer, and the scent is on the strong side. Its twiggy, arching growth is very prickly and the grey-green leaves are small and ferny. It is highly effective in a free, informal scheme. Remove diseased, dead, and damaged growth, but leave the old wood intact. A minimal late-winter prune also helps produce a balanced shape.

PLANT PROFILE

HEIGHT	90cm (3ft)
SPREAD	1.2m (4ft)
TYPE	Wild
HARDINESS	Fully hardy
FLOWERING	Summer to autumn

SUMMER WINE ('Korinzont')

S

THE CORAL-PINK, SCENTED FLOWERS, with a dash of red in the centre, appear on stiff, branching, upright growth, which should easily cover a medium-size wall, even in shade. SUMMER WINE can also be trained up and round pillars, posts, and arches. Training the stems into the horizontal (if possible) forces up even more flowering growth. The display lasts all summer. From the third year prune in the autumn after flowering, nipping back overlong main stems and shortening sideshoots by two-thirds.

PLANT PROFILE	
HEIGHT 3m (10ft)	
TYPE Climber	
HARDINESS Fully hardy	
FLOWERING Summer to autumn	

S SUNBLEST ('Landora')

A FIRST-RATE, ALL-PURPOSE, BRIGHT YELLOW ROSE, it has a compact shape, reliably flowers all summer, and provides plenty of cut stems. Each bloom is on the large side, at 9cm (3½in) wide, has pointed petals, and is set against a background of glossy leaves. There might be occasional attacks of black spot, but that certainly should not deter amateur growers. In late winter remove all unproductive stems, and prune the rest hard to outward-facing buds at 20–25cm (8–10in). This helps keep the centre clear of crossing shoots. For large, showy flowers prune harder, leaving just two or three buds.

PLANT PROFILE

HEIGHT 90cm (3ft)

SPREAD 60cm (24in)

TYPE Bush (large-flowered)

HARDINESS Fully hardy

FLOWERING Summer to autumn

SUNSET BOULEVARD ('Harbabble')

S

VOTED UK ROSE OF THE YEAR IN 1997, SUNSET BOULEVARD is a high-quality, compact plant with attractive buds producing warm pink flowers. There is almost no let-up in the show over summer and, despite the lack of scent, its other qualities make it an excellent choice for gaps right at the front of a border. Do not crowd it too much with adjacent plants or the stylish, shapely flowers might well get obscured. In late winter cut back the main stems to approximately 25–45cm (10–18in) above ground, and shorten the sideshoots by about one third.

PLANT PROFILE	
HEIGHT 90cm (3ft)	
SPREAD 60cm (24in)	
TYPE Bush (cluster-flowered)	
HARDINESS Fully hardy	
FLOWERING Summer to autumn	

S | SURREY ('Korlanum')

ONE OF THE MOST EFFECTIVE ground-cover roses, SURREY covers a decent area with a mound of dense, leafy growth and stems. Hardly any weeds will grow through it. The flowering is equally good, with warm pink blooms all summer and a nice scent. It makes a very effective low shape in front of taller plants. In very large gardens you can even use it in spreading drifts. Minimal pruning is needed, but if growth is getting too rampant, cut back the main shoots to outward-facing buds in late winter and reduce sideshoots at the same time.

PLANT PROFILE

HEIGHT 80cm (32in)

SPREAD 1.2m (4ft)

TYPE Ground-cover

HARDINESS Fully hardy

FLOWERING Summer to autumn

SWANY ('Meiburenac')

S

MAKE SURE THAT YOU HAVE ROOM for SWANY's vigorous, dense, ground-cover growth, packed with glossy, dark green leaves. It is too big a spreader for borders but will effectively block out weeds on a sunny, spare patch of ground. There are profuse clusters of small white flowers all summer, though you will have to get very close to notice any scent. Little pruning is needed. If growth is too rampant, cut back the main and sideshoots to outward-facing buds in late winter.

PLANT PROFILE	
HEIGHT 75cm (30in)	
SPREAD To 1.7m (5½ft)	
TYPE Ground-cover	
HARDINESS Fully hardy	
FLOWERING Summer to autumn	

SWEET DREAM ('Fryminicot')

THE ROSE BREEDERS' ROSE OF THE YEAR in 1988, it is still a top buy, with a range of virtues. SWEET DREAM has a gorgeous peach–apricot colour that does not fade, the flowers are good at withstanding the rain, and there is neat, leafy, bushy growth. You can grow this versatile patio rose where you want – in pots, at the foot of tall structures or ornamental objects, or to encircle larger feature plants. In late winter cut out all growth apart from the strongest shoots, and then cut them back by about one-third to one-half. This regime forces up plenty of new, vigorous growth.

PLANT PROFILE

HEIGHT 40cm (16in)

SPREAD 35cm (14in)

TYPE Bush (cluster-flowered, patio)

HARDINESS Fully hardy

FLOWERING Summer to autumn

SWEET JULIET ('Ausleap')

S

COMBINING OLD GARDEN ROSE–TYPE FLOWERS with plenty of vigour, SWEET JULIET has fresh buds all summer long, producing a lovely show of apricot-yellow flowers. New growth has a tendency to appear just about anywhere, including right at the base, creating a dense tangle of stems. All this energetic growth invariably means more stems than flowers, but heavy pruning redresses the balance. The leaves are long and pointed. In late winter prune stems by one-half to two-thirds. Harder pruning gives fewer stems with larger flowers, and lighter pruning more stems with smaller blooms.

PLANT PROFILE

HEIGHT	1.2m (4ft)
SPREAD	90cm (3ft)
TYPE	Shrub
HARDINESS	Fully hardy
FLOWERING	Summer to autumn

S SWEET MAGIC ('Dicmagic')

THE ROYAL NATIONAL ROSE SOCIETY voted this Rose of the Year in 1987. It has an excellent supply of apricot-orange flowers (with a dash of yellow, which increases as the flowers fade), set against bright green leaves. Hips follow the flowers. It looks equally good whether grown in pots, as edging, or right at the front of a border. You do not have to be green-fingered to grow SWEET MAGIC. In late winter remove all growth apart from the strongest shoots, and cut these back by one-third to one-half. This regime forces up plenty of new, vigorous, twiggy growth.

PLANT PROFILE

HEIGHT 45cm (18in)

SPREAD 45cm (18in)

TYPE Bush (cluster-flowered, patio)

HARDINESS Fully hardy

FLOWERING Summer to autumn; hips in autumn

'Sympathie'

S

THE FIRST FLUSH OF FLOWERS is the best, producing deep, dark red blooms in heavy clusters. They are borne on free-branching, arching stems covered with dark green leaves. More flowers follow and compensate for the lack of scent. It is equally successful against walls and growing over arches. For the first two years train new shoots into a horizontal position to produce flowering sideshoots. From the third year prune in the autumn, after flowering, nipping back the main stems if necessary and shortening sideshoots by two-thirds.

PLANT PROFILE	
HEIGHT 3m (10ft)	
TYPE Climber	
HARDINESS Fully hardy	
FLOWERING Summer to autumn	

T TANGO ('Macfirwal')

ALSO KNOWN AS STRETCH JOHNSON, TANGO is a highly
distinctive rose. The flowers are bright orange-red, with yellow
in the centre and yellowish-white round the rim of the petals.
The ebullient effect (a bit over the top for some) is enhanced
because the flowers appear in large clusters. Make sure it suits
your colour scheme. Introduced in 1988, it promptly won a
Royal National Rose Society Gold Medal. Cut back the main
stems in late winter to 25–45cm (10–18in), and shorten
sideshoots by about one-third.

PLANT PROFILE	
HEIGHT	75cm (30in)
SPREAD	60cm (24in)
TYPE	Bush (cluster-flowered)
HARDINESS	Fully hardy
FLOWERING	Summer to autumn

TEQUILA SUNRISE ('Dicobey')

T

A FLASHY, POPULAR, BRIGHTLY COLOURED ROSE, it has sprays of 10cm (4in) wide, yellow flowers with scarlet running along the top tips of the petals. They keep going through the summer. Growth is quite bushy and vigorous, and the leaves are glossy, dark green. If you need an eye-catching rose at the front of the border, put it high on your list. In late winter remove all the unproductive stems, and prune the rest hard to outward-facing buds at 20–25cm (8–10in). This helps remove crisscrossing shoots in the centre. For large, showy flowers prune harder, to just two or three buds.

PLANT PROFILE	
HEIGHT	75cm (30in)
SPREAD	60cm (24in)
TYPE	Bush (large-flowered)
HARDINESS	Fully hardy
FLOWERING	Summer to autumn

T | 'The Fairy'

'THE FAIRY' HAS EVERYTHING GOING FOR IT, except that flowering does not begin until the second half of summer. If you can wait, you get wonderfully bushy, moundy growth covered by clusters of tiny buds that open to small, light pink flowers giving an informal, cottage-garden show. It can be grown as a shrub, hedge, or even in a large tub. It is also highly effective as a standard. When pruning remove only diseased, dead, and damaged growth. A minimal late-winter prune also helps produce a balanced shape. If you want fewer stems with larger flowers, prune harder.

PLANT PROFILE

HEIGHT 60–90cm (24–36in)

SPREAD 60–90cm (24–36in)

TYPE Shrub

HARDINESS Fully hardy

FLOWERING Late summer to autumn

'The Garland'

T

AN OLD, IMPRESSIVE RAMBLER, dating back to 1835, it has a strong, fruity scent. The once-a-summer profusion of pinkish-white buds opens to small, white, flat flowers with a yellow eye. They look a bit like daisies and make a terrific display, standing out against the almost dark green leaves. 'The Garland' can be grown up the trunks of old stout trees, or allowed to pile up, making a big, baggy informal shrub. In late summer, for the first two years, prune sideshoots by 8cm (3in) to a strong new shoot. From the thrid year, prune at most one-third of the oldest main stems back to ground level.

PLANT PROFILE	
HEIGHT	5m (15ft)
TYPE	Rambler
HARDINESS	Fully hardy
FLOWERING	Midsummer

T | THE PILGRIM ('Auswalker')

IF YOU LIKE THE YELLOW ROSE GRAHAM THOMAS (*see page 135*), you may also want THE PILGRIM, which was raised from it. There is a lovely mix of scented, soft yellow flowers, pale in the centre and almost white around the outside. The look is of an old garden rose, but the vigour matches a modern one. Growth is nicely upright, and it can also be trained as a modest climber, reaching 2.5m (8ft). In late winter prune stems by one-half to two-thirds. Harder pruning gives fewer stems with larger flowers, and lighter pruning more stems with smaller blooms.

PLANT PROFILE

HEIGHT 1.1m (3½ft)

SPREAD 90cm (3ft)

TYPE Shrub

HARDINESS Fully hardy

FLOWERING Summer

'The Queen Elizabeth'

T

ALSO KNOWN SIMPLY AS QUEEN ELIZABETH, this is one bush rose that definitely needs to go right at the back of the border because it shoots up over head-height. The leaves are impressively large, leathery, dark green and glossy, and the whole plant is so sturdy and upright that it can also be grown as a decent hedge. It was voted the World's Favourite Rose in 1979 and remains a top-class plant. In late winter cut back the main stems to 25–45cm (10–18in) above ground, and shorten the sideshoots by about two-thirds.

PLANT PROFILE

HEIGHT	To 2.2m (7ft)
SPREAD	90cm (3ft)
TYPE	Bush (cluster-flowered)
HARDINESS	Fully hardy
FLOWERING	Summer to autumn

T | THE TIMES ROSE ('Korpeahn')

FOR A REGULAR SUPPLY OF CRIMSON FLOWERS all summer
on a modest-sized, disease-resistant bush rose, this takes
some beating. The colour is bright, and the dark green
leaves (reddish-bronze when young) provide an effective
background. Plant it at the foot of a pergola with climbers
shooting up past it, at the front of a border, or wherever you
need an attention-grabbing rose. In late winter cut back the
main stems to 25–45cm (10–18in), and reduce the sideshoots
by about one-third of their length.

PLANT PROFILE	
HEIGHT	60cm (24in)
SPREAD	75cm (30in)
TYPE	Bush (cluster-flowered)
HARDINESS	Fully hardy
FLOWERING	Summer to autumn

Top Marks ('Fryministar')

CHOCK-A-BLOCK WITH SMALL, VERMILION FLOWERS, this compact plant has a huge presence and was voted UK Rose of the Year in 1992. The flowers hang on well, keeping their intense colour, but if you really want them to stand out, plant TOP MARKS in a pot, giving it a prominent position. It is also excellent in patio gardens and for edging paths. The leaves are glossy and healthy. In late winter remove all growth apart from the strongest shoots, and then cut them back by one-third to one-half. This forces up plenty of new, vigorous growth.

PLANT PROFILE

HEIGHT 45cm (18in)

SPREAD 45cm (18in)

TYPE Bush (cluster-flowered, patio)

HARDINESS Fully hardy

FLOWERING Summer

T | 'Tour de Malakoff'

IF YOU ARE CREATING AN OLD ROSE GARDEN specializing in large flowers and good scent, try this. The flowers are 12cm (5in) wide and well scented, initially with a mix of purple and red (and a dash of gold in the middle), then turning violet and grey. A fine old Centifolia rose, dating back to 1856, it has arching growth that often needs support. When pruning remove only diseased, dead, and damaged growth, and leave the old wood. A minimal late-winter prune yields a balanced shape and more stems with smaller blooms, while harder pruning gives fewer stems with larger flowers.

PLANT PROFILE

HEIGHT 2m (6ft)

SPREAD 1.5m (5ft)

TYPE Old garden rose

HARDINESS Fully hardy

FLOWERING Midsummer

TROIKA ('Poumidor')

SOMETIMES KNOWN AS ROYAL DANE, this has large, 15cm (6in) wide, nicely scented flowers with a high centre. The colour is showy and eye-catching, a good choice for bright and brash schemes, or for the focal point in a quieter scheme. Growth is vigorous and tall, with glossy, dark green leaves, making a perfectly reliable rose. In late winter remove all the unproductive stems, and prune the rest hard to outward-facing buds, leaving 20–25cm (8–10in) of stem. This helps eliminate crossing shoots in the centre of the bush. For large, showy flowers prune harder, leaving just two or three buds.

T

PLANT PROFILE	
HEIGHT 90cm (3ft)	
SPREAD 75cm (30in)	
TYPE Bush (large-flowered)	
HARDINESS Fully hardy	
FLOWERING Summer to autumn	

T

TRUMPETER ('Mactru')

A LIVELY BLAST OF TOMATO ORANGE-RED FLOWERS lasts all summer, into autumn. Growth is neat and compact, with a nice backing of rich, green foliage, and disease is not a problem. TRUMPETER scores high marks at the front of a border where it can be clearly seen. It can also be grown in a circle around an ornamental object (such as a classical, formal staute), or in rows to flank the edge of a path. In late winter cut back the main stems to 25–45cm (10–18in), and reduce the sideshoots by about one-third of their length.

PLANT PROFILE

HEIGHT	60cm (24in)
SPREAD	50cm (20in)
TYPE	Bush (cluster-flowered)
HARDINESS	Fully hardy
FLOWERING	Summer to autumn

'Tuscany Superb' Double velvet rose

T

THE DEEP, RICH RED VELVETY PETALS, gradually fading to purple, make this a wonderful rose, especially as there is a dash of gold in the eye of the flowers. Growth is relatively thornless, strong, and bushy. It is often listed under Gallica roses in catalogues. When pruning, remove only diseased, dead, and damaged growth, and leave the old wood. Give it a minimal late-winter prune for a balanced shape. The harder you prune, the fewer the stems and the larger the flowers, while lighter pruning gives more stems with smaller blooms.

PLANT PROFILE	
HEIGHT	90cm (3ft)
SPREAD	90cm (3ft)
TYPE	Old garden rose
HARDINESS	Fully hardy
FLOWERING	Midsummer

V | VALENCIA ('Koreklia')

BETTER IN A COTTAGE OR INFORMAL GARDEN because of its slightly uneven, sprawling growth, VALENCIA scores high marks for its large, 10cm (4in) wide, scented flowers. The high-centred, long-stemmed flowers (excellent for cutting) have a hint of copper, and are nicely set off by the leathery, glossy, dark green leaves. The display lasts into autumn. In late winter prune out all the unproductive stems, and cut the rest back to outward-facing buds at 20–25cm (8–10in). This helps deter crossing shoots in the centre. For large, showy flowers prune to just two or three buds.

PLANT PROFILE

HEIGHT	75cm (30in)
SPREAD	65cm (26in)
TYPE	Bush (large-flowered)
HARDINESS	Fully hardy
FLOWERING	Summer to autumn

VALENTINE HEART ('Dicogle')

V

THE BUDS SUGGEST SCARLET FLOWERS but they actually turn out to be pink with a hint of lilac, and have distinctive, frilly petals. The leaves are purple when young, and then turn dark green. The effect is of a small, beautiful, free-and-easy display just right for the front of a bed where its growth can edge on to a path. The long summer show means it is well worth buying several plants, and lining them up in a row. In late winter cut back the main stems to 25–45cm (10–18in), and reduce sideshoots by one-third of their length.

PLANT PROFILE

HEIGHT 60cm (24in)

SPREAD 50cm (20in)

TYPE Bush (cluster-flowered)

HARDINESS Fully hardy

FLOWERING Summer to autumn

V 'Variegata di Bologna'

OFTEN CALLED A STRIPED ROSE, this has a creamy-white flower with reddish markings and stripes in an irregular pattern, like a great big dollop of raspberry-ripple ice cream. There is just one show of flowers, well worth waiting for and never too garish. Growth is quite strong and vigorous, which means it can be trained as a short climber. 'Variegata di Bologna' is often listed as a Bourbon rose in catalogues. To create a large shrub remove only diseased, dead, and damaged growth, and leave the old wood intact. A minimal late-winter prune helps to create a balanced shape.

PLANT PROFILE	
HEIGHT 2.2m (7ft)	
SPREAD 1.5m (5ft)	
TYPE Old garden rose	
HARDINESS Fully hardy	
FLOWERING Summer to autumn	

'Veilchenblau'

A BIG HIT WITH ROSE EXPERTS, this has thornless stems
and sprays of small, scented flowers that change colour. The
buds are reddish-purple, and the opening flowers are maroon-
purple with white. They turn bluish-lilac and fade to lilac-grey
on about the third day. 'Veilchenblau' needs the right
background to stand out, and will be lost against the likes of
a grey stone wall. Try growing it up a pergola with a rich red,
and a white climber. For the first two years prune sideshoots
by 8cm (3in) to a strong shoot in late summer. From the third
year prune up to one-third of the oldest stems to the ground.

PLANT PROFILE

HEIGHT 4m (12ft)

TYPE Rambler

HARDINESS Fully hardy

FLOWERING Midsummer

V | *virginiana*

FROM NORTH AMERICA, the wild *R. virginiana* tolerates most soils, including the light and sandy. It makes bushy, shrubby growth and is thick with glossy leaves, producing clear pink, scented flowers. It is at its best in the autumn, when the leaves turn beetroot-red as the cold comes, changing to yellow-orange. There is also a good show of round, orange hips. Give it a prominent position. Remove only diseased, dead, and damaged growth, and leave the old wood intact. A minimal late-winter prune helps to promote a balanced shape.

PLANT PROFILE

HEIGHT 1.2m (4ft)

SPREAD 1.2m (4ft)

TYPE Wild

HARDINESS Fully hardy

FLOWERING Midsummer; hips in autumn

WARM WELCOME ('Chewizz')

W

THIS BELONGS TO THE GROUP of modest climbers that are ideal for small walls, or short pillars and posts. The clusters of small flowers cover the plant from top to bottom, giving a good show right through the summer months, while its disease-resistant leaves have a glossy shine. WARM WELCOME can be pruned to restrict height, but will react by putting up more climbing shoots right from the base, making the rose much bushier. It is best to leave well alone. Train the new shoots horizontally to produce plenty of flowering sideshoots.

PLANT PROFILE	
HEIGHT	2.2m (7ft)
TYPE	Climber
HARDINESS	Fully hardy
FLOWERING	Summer to autumn

W | WARM WISHES ('Fryxotic')

A FAILSAFE CHOICE for a warm peachy colour, this rose is well
known for its ability to keep flowering over summer and
withstand the worst of the weather. In other countries it goes
by the name of SUNSET CELEBRATION, a good indication of its
colour. Growth is strong and bushy, with dark green leaves.
Position it in gaps at the front of the border or in a special
rose scheme. Remove all the unproductive stems in late
winter, and prune the rest hard to outward–facing buds at
20–25cm (8–10in). For large, showy flowers prune harder,
leaving just two or three buds.

PLANT PROFILE

HEIGHT 75cm (30in)

SPREAD 60cm (24in)

TYPE Bush (large-flowered)

HARDINESS Fully hardy

FLOWERING Summer

'Wedding Day'

W

A GIANT OF A RAMBLER, it needs a huge, stout tree to scramble up, or let it loose in a hedgerow. It is a fine sight in midsummer, with its large clusters of opening, yellowish buds, followed by wonderfully citrus-scented, creamy-white small flowers with yellow in the centre. 'Wedding Day' is a better version than its parent, which was found wild in China. Do not be surprised if its exceeds its suggested growth by another 3m (10ft). In late summer, for the first two years, prune sideshoots by 8cm (3in) to a new shoot. From the third year, prune up to one-third of the old main stems to ground level.

PLANT PROFILE

HEIGHT 8m (25ft)

TYPE Rambler

HARDINESS Fully hardy

FLOWERING Midsummer

W | WEE JOCK ('Cocabest')

SMALL AND COMPACT, this has two key selling points. The buds are high-pointed, and the petal-packed flowers are deep crimson. They are not that prolific, appearing in reasonable-sized clusters, but the colour is so strong that WEE JOCK immediately grabs the eye. It can be used as edging, or placed at the front of a border. It is also good choice for brightening up sunny courtyard gardens. In late winter remove all growth apart from the strongest shoots, and then cut them back by one-third to one-half. This regime forces up plenty of new, vigorous growth.

PLANT PROFILE	
HEIGHT 35cm (14in)	
SPREAD 35cm (14in)	
TYPE Bush (cluster-flowered, miniature)	
HARDINESS Fully hardy	
FLOWERING Summer to autumn	

WESTERLAND ('Korwest')

A VIGOROUS, STIFF-STEMMED, UPRIGHT SHRUB, this can also be trained against a wall as a climber, when it can reach 2.5m (8ft) high. Its clusters of scented flowers are brightly coloured, with a touch of yellow, and there is barely any let-up over summer. The leaves are dark green. If you grow it as a climber, try to put it against a white wall to bring out the contrast of dark green leaves and orange flowers. To create a large shrub, remove diseased, dead, and damaged growth, and prune lightly for shape in late winter. Harder pruning gives fewer stems with larger flowers.

PLANT PROFILE	
HEIGHT	2m (6ft)
SPREAD	1.2m (4ft)
TYPE	Shrub
HARDINESS	Fully hardy
FLOWERING	Summer to autumn

W

WHISKY MAC ('Tanky')

ITS BEAUTIFUL MERGING OF YELLOWISH-GOLD and amber petals stands out in the border like a flame against its dark green leaves. The scent is mild, the flowers large at 10cm (4in) wide, and the only possible setback is that it is on the tender side; a sunny, sheltered site and good soil are vital. Some say it is unreliable after a few years, but the best advice is to have a go because it really is quite special. In late winter remove all unproductive stems, and prune the rest hard to outward-facing buds at 20–25cm (8–10in). This helps remove crisscrossing shoots. For larger flowers prune to two or three buds.

PLANT PROFILE	
HEIGHT	75cm (30in)
SPREAD	60cm (24in)
TYPE	Bush (large-flowered)
HARDINESS	Frost hardy
FLOWERING	Summer to autumn

'White Cockade'

W

A THOROUGHLY RESTRAINED CLIMBER, 'White Cockade' has beautifully shaped white flowers, excellent for cutting. The scent is mild. Growth is on the shrubby side, with dark green leaves, giving good coverage against a smallish wall. 'White Cockade' is also a smart choice for growing up round the legs of a pergola. For the first two years train new shoots into a horizontal position to produce flowering sideshoots. From then on prune in the autumn, after flowering, nipping back overlong main stems, and shortening sideshoots by two-thirds.

PLANT PROFILE	
HEIGHT 2.2m (7ft)	
TYPE Climber	
HARDINESS Fully hardy	
FLOWERING Summer to autumn	

W | 'William Lobb'

THIS MOSS ROSE DOES A QUICK COLOUR CHANGE: the flowers open deep, rich purple but, within a day, are lavender-grey, giving the whole shrub a two-tone appearance. Because of its rich scent, it is better grown in a sheltered spot where the smell hangs in the air. It makes a good companion in most schemes with its arching stems, and can even be grown against a sunny wall. Remove only diseased, dead, and damaged growth. A minimal late-winter prune also helps produce a balanced shape and plenty of flowering stems with smaller blooms. Harder pruning gives fewer stems with larger flowers.

PLANT PROFILE	
HEIGHT	2m (6ft)
SPREAD	2m (6ft)
TYPE	Old garden rose
HARDINESS	Fully hardy
FLOWERING	Early summer

WINCHESTER CATHEDRAL ('Auscat')

W

WITH THE LOOKS OF AN OLD GARDEN ROSE and the vigour of a modern shrub, this is a first-rate alternative to the related pink MARY ROSE (*see page 188*), the one difference being that it is white. The most appropriate setting for it is in a cottage garden because of its old-world charm. Growth is twiggy, bushy, and uneven, and perfectly disease-resistant. The flowers will not win any prizes on the show-bench, but cannot be faulted as part of a general scheme. There is repeat-flowering and a light, barely discernible scent. Prune stems in late winter by one-half to two-thirds.

PLANT PROFILE	
HEIGHT 1.2m (4ft)	
SPREAD 1.2m (4ft)	
TYPE Shrub	
HARDINESS Fully hardy	
FLOWERING Summer	

X | *xanthina* 'Canary Bird'

THIS NEEDS TO BE GROWN in wild or informal gardens where there is room for its arching tangle of growth. With luck there may be some later flowers, but most invariably appear in spring, making it one of the earliest roses to flower. 'Canary Bird' (which is how it is sometimes listed in catalogues) is slightly larger than the related *R. xanthina*, which also has yellow flowers in the spring. It is thorny and large, requiring plenty of space. Remove only diseased, dead, and damaged growth, and leave the old wood intact. A light trim in late winter helps to produce a balanced shape.

PLANT PROFILE	
HEIGHT 3m (10ft)	
SPREAD To 4m (12ft)	
TYPE Shrub	
HARDINESS Fully hardy	
FLOWERING Late spring	

xanthina f. *hugonis* Golden rose of China

X

AT 2M (6FT) HIGH AND WIDE, it makes much less intrusive, shrubby growth than the very similar *R. xanthina* 'Canary Bird', and is a better bet for more modest hedgerows and perimeter planting. The flowers are on the pale yellow side. It is sometimes known just as *R. hugonis* (Father Hugo's rose). When pruning remove only the diseased, dead, and damaged growth, and leave the old wood intact. A minimal late-winter prune yields a better shape, though it will never be neat.

PLANT PROFILE	
HEIGHT	2m (6ft)
SPREAD	2m (6ft)
TYPE	Wild
HARDINESS	Fully hardy
FLOWERING	Late spring

Z | 'Zéphirine Drouhin' Thornless rose

A FAVOURITE SINCE 1868, this Bourbon rose has thorn-free growth, rich green leaves, and a lavish show of sweet-scented, cerise-pink flowers all summer. With pruning, it forms a large shrub, but it can also be grown as a climber, reaching up to 4m (12ft) high. It can even make a hedge, and flowers (less prolifically) on a cold, shady wall. In late winter prune the stems by one-half to two-thirds to produce a shrubby bush. Harder pruning gives fewer stems with larger flowers, while lighter pruning gives more stems with smaller blooms.

PLANT PROFILE	
HEIGHT To 2.5m (8ft)	
SPREAD 2m (6ft)	
TYPE Old garden rose	
HARDINESS Fully hardy	
FLOWERING Summer to autumn	

'Zigeunerknabe'

Z

ALSO CALLED GIPSY BOY, this rose makes a small climber with strong, prickly, arching stems. It can also be grown as a large shrub when gently pruned. The flowers are superb. They have a deep, dark colour highlighted by the gold stamens. The leaves might be coarse and dark green but they are certainly disease-resistant. If you have a less-than-ideal place for a rose, this should succeed. It is sometimes listed with Bourbon roses in catalogues. In late winter cut back stems by one-half to two-thirds, pruning harder for fewer stems with larger flowers, and more lightly for more stems with smaller blooms.

PLANT PROFILE

HEIGHT 2m (6ft)

SPREAD 1.2m (4ft)

TYPE Old garden rose

HARDINESS Fully hardy

FLOWERING Early summer

Rose suppliers

You should find a large number of the roses in this book at garden centres but, for more unusual varieties, try these specialist nurseries.

Acton Beauchamp Roses
Acton Beauchamp, Worcester,
Worcestershire WR6 5AE
Tel: (01531) 640433

Battersby Roses
1 Peartree Cottages, Battersby,
Great Ayton, North Yorkshire TS9 6LU
Tel: (01642) 723402
www.battersbyroses.8m.com

Burrows Roses
Meadow Croft, Spondon Road, Dale
Abbey, Derby, Derbyshire DE7 4PQ
Tel: (01332) 668289

C & K Jones
Golden Fields Nursery, Barrow Lane,
Tarvin, Cheshire CH3 8JF
Tel: (01829) 740663
www.jonestherose.co.uk

Cants of Colchester
Nayland Road, Mile End,
Colchester, Essex CO4 5EB
Tel: (01206) 844008
www.cantsroses.co.uk

Cley Nurseries Ltd
Holt Road, Cley-next-the-Sea,
Holt, Norfolk NR25 7TX
Tel: (01263) 740892

David Austin Roses Ltd
Bowling Green Lane, Albrighton,
Wolverhampton WV7 3HB
Tel: (01902) 376377
www.davidaustinroses.com

Dickson Nurseries Ltd
42a Milecross Road, Newtownards,
Co. Down, N. Ireland BT23 4SS
Tel: (028) 9181 2206
www.dickson-roses.co.uk

Fryer's Nurseries Ltd
Manchester Road, Knutsford,
Cheshire, WA16 0SX
Tel: (01565) 755455
www.fryers-roses.co.uk

Gandy's (Roses) Ltd
North Kilworth, Nr Lutterworth,
Leicestershire LE17 6HZ
Tel: (01858) 880398

Greenhead Roses
Greenhead Nursery,
Old Greenock Road, Inchinnan,
Renfrew, Scotland PA4 9PH
Tel: (0141) 812 0121

Henry Street Nursery
Swallowfield Road, Arborfield,
Reading, Berkshire RG2 9JY
Tel: (0118) 976 1223
www.henrystreet.co.uk

Hunts Court Garden & Nursery
North Nibley, Dursley,
Gloucestershire GL11 6DZ
Tel: (01453) 547440

Iain Brodie of Falsyde
Cuilalunn, Kinchurdy Road,
Boat of Garten, Invernesshire,
Scotland PH24 3BP
Tel: (01479) 831464

James Cocker & Sons
Whitemyres, Lang Stracht, Aberdeen,
Scotland AB15 6XH
Tel: (01224) 313261
www.roses.uk.com

Mattock's Roses
The Rose Nurseries, Nuneham
Courtenay, Oxford OX44 9PY
Tel: 08457 585652
www.mattocks.co.uk

The Old Vicarage Nursery
Lucton, Leominster,
Herefordshire HR6 9PN
Tel: (01568) 780538

Perryhill Nurseries Ltd
Hartfield,
East Sussex TN7 4JP
Tel: (01892) 770377
www.perryhillnurseries.co.uk

Peter Beales Roses
London Road, Attleborough,
Norwich, Norfolk NR17 1AY
Tel: (01953) 454707
www.classicroses.co.uk

Seale Nurseries
Seale Lane, Seale, Farnham,
Surrey GU10 1LD
Tel: (01252) 782410
www.sealesuperroses.com

Trevor White Old Fashioned Roses
Bennetts Brier, The Street, Felthorpe,
Norwich, Norfolk NR10 4AB
Tel: (01603) 755135

Wych Cross Nurseries
Wych Cross, Forest Row,
East Sussex RH18 5JW
Tel: (01342) 822705
www.wychcross.co.uk

The publisher would like to thank the following for their kind permission to reproduce their photographs:

a=above; c=centre; b=below; l=left; r=right t=top;

21: Photos Horticultural; 27: Roger Smith/DK; 44: Roger Smith/DK; 53: Roger Smith/DK; 56: (both) Roger Smith/DK; 57: Photos Horticultural; 69: Garden Picture Library/David Askham; 83: Roger Smith/DK; 87: Photos Horticultural; 114: Photos Horticultural; 118: Roger Smith/DK; 126: Roger Smith/DK; 154: Photos Horticultural; 159: Garden Picture Library/David Askhan; 160: Roger Smith/DK; 166: Roger Smith/DK; 169: Clive Nichols; 181: Garden and Wildlife Matters/J.Vere Brown; 182: Garden and Wildlife Matters/Steffie Shields; 194: Garden Picture Library/ Elizabeth Crowe; 200: Garden and Wildlife Matters/Steffie Shields; 207: Garden Picture Library/Densey Clyn; 210: Kordes Rosen; 213: Clive Nichols; 215: Andrew Lawson; 219: Garden Picture Library/Laslo Puskas; 235: Photos Horticultural; 253: (both) Roger Smith/DK; 254: (both) Roger Smith/DK; 260: Roger Smith/DK; 264: Roger Smith/DK; 269: Photos Horticultural; 275: Roger Smith/DK; 279: Roger Smith/DK; 300: Roger Smith/DK; 302: (main) Roger Smith/DK; 303: Roger Smith/DK; 304: Garden and Wildlife Matters; 305: Garden Picture Library/Brigitte Thomas; 307: Clive Nichols; 313: Andrew Lawson.

All other images © Dorling Kindersley.

For further information see: www.dkimages.com